Journaling
with
JEREMIAH

ELIZABETH CANHAM

PAULIST PRESS
New York/Mahwah, N.J.

"The Ballad of Joe Hill" by Judy Russell and Gary Revel was published by The House of Talley Music Co. All rights reserved. The excerpt from *The Discipline of the Mountain* by Daniel Berrigan, and the poem "A Trilogy of Love," from *As Tentative as Flight* by Peter J. Ediger, are reprinted by permission of the authors.

Library of Congress Cataloging-in-Publication Data

Canham, Elizabeth, 1939–
    Journaling with Jeremiah / Elizabeth J. Canham.
      p. cm.
    ISBN 0-8091-3334-2
    1. Bible. O.T. Jeremiah—Devotional use.   2. Spiritual journals—Authorship.   3. Jeremiah (Biblical prophet)   I. Title.
    BS1525.5.C364   1992
    224'.206—dc20   92-16467
                                                              CIP

Published by Paulist Press
997 Macarthur Blvd.
Mahwah N.J. 07430

Printed and bound in the United States of America

Contents

Introduction

During my childhood in England I was blessed with a mother who was a superb story teller. Night after night she read to us, entering into the tales and sharing her own enthusiasm for the characters who fired our imaginations. One of my favorite books was *Winnie the Pooh* by A.A. Milne. I loved the vulnerable, loveable and sometimes naive bear who lumbered along getting himself into some tight places as he risked new adventures, always trusting in the basic goodness of life. I loved Eyeore, the rather gloomy donkey who always expected the worst. He had a pretty low self-image and was often overcome by paranoia. Perhaps I loved them most because they reflect and affirm aspects of my own personality and life story.

The prophet Jeremiah has also been a friend and companion for several years, supporting and challenging my own journey with God. The emotions he experienced, the questions he asked and the world in which he lived bear a strong resemblance to mine even though our life history is separated by two and a half thousand years. This man of God continues to give inspiration through his faith, and hope through his humanity. Sometimes he does seem very gloomy and, like Eyeore, he complains, expects disaster, and has a low view of his own worth. Yet despite all the afflictions he suffers, a robust faith in God's goodness surfaces again and again. He keeps on stepping out, going on, picking himself up and expending his energy to inspire hope in others just as Pooh did.

The purpose of this book is to share my friendship with Jeremiah and to suggest the relevance of his life and message to those of us trying to live as God's people today. We too inhabit a tumultuous world in which crumbling power structures and economic inequity are fearful realities demanding our prayer and action. We find ourselves constantly called to new beginnings, and fresh visions of hope as we relinquish the old security blankets of tradition and find shocking new ways to startle ourselves and others into a more radical obedience to the Word of God. Jeremiah affirms us, supports us, tells us that, even as our cry of anguish is heard by God, we come to know that the Creator struggles with us in the darkness.

The integrity of Jeremiah and his message challenges any inclination we may have to compromise or minimize the demands of the Gospel. The prophet truly embodied the word of God at a time when people had grown deaf to the voice of Yahweh. He was not popular with the political or religious establishment because he exposed complacency and stood as God's spokesperson in public places. Our own call to live prophetically is underscored by his life, and the strength to persevere comes for us too as we struggle with fear and allow hope to take root deep within us. This note of hope is sounded often by Jeremiah, especially as he ministers to God's people in exile. Because he was willing to live through the isolating consequences of his obedience to God, he could empathize with those cut off from their homeland and even encourage them to find blessing in their tenuous existence. Our journey also takes us through some times of instability when loss and rootlessness cause us to feel abandoned by the God we try to serve. Then the promises of new life and community echo down the centuries, enabling us to be where we are and to know God in the precariousness of life.

In an age which offers a diet of bland religion the message of Jeremiah adds a piquant edge to the palate. It refuses to be contained within the narrow confines of exclusivism for God is the Lord of Hosts and nations. We are compelled to think globally as we share our faith in a pluralistic society and this often means dealing with a great deal of ambiguity and giving up the craving for the certainty that finds security in a ghetto mentality. Our prayer must take place in the marketplace, addressing the issues that confront men and women today, and finding our identity with them in their struggles for justice. Jeremiah stands alongside us to nerve our endeavour and to remind us that God is awake, watching over all our ways, to bring about the divine purpose through our obedience.

Journaling with Jeremiah seeks to bring together two of the most important resources available to us as we pray: Scripture and our capacity to reflect on and dialogue with the Word of God. The Bible is alive, contemporary, and vibrantly available to each one of us, though we may not know it! The process of reading, digesting, and entering into the story of God's people as told in Scripture is a process of self-discovery and of a deepening awareness of who God is for us. The journaling method suggested in this book facilitates that process and takes us deeper into conversation with the Lord who creates, loves, calls and enables us. As we journal, and journey, we give voice to the many experiences that afflict, fortify and form us in companionship with those ancestors of the faith who found the courage to tell their stories. Of these forebears

Jeremiah is, perhaps, the most honest and vulnerable, willing to share his doubts and reveal his deepest longings. He touches us and lights the way by his faithful, daily commitment to the God who precipitates him into compassionate action.

Elizabeth J. Canham

Preface:
Journaling—A Way To Pray

*I*n the Christian tradition, journal keeping has a long history. The Confessions of St. Augustine, St. Teresa's autobiography, the journals of Pope John XXIII, Thomas Merton, Henri Nouwen—all testify to the value of keeping a personal journal. Nor is this practice confined to clergy and religious in the Catholic tradition. The moving little book *Markings,* containing reflections on the personal faith journey of the former Secretary General of the United Nations, Dag Hammarskjöld, invites us to see how Christian discipleship may be lived in a world where fear, violence, oppression and the threat of nuclear holocaust are realities. Dietrich Bonhoeffer has left us an account of his struggle, written from the cell in Nazi Germany which was his world until his untimely execution a few days before the end of the European conflict in World War II. All of these, and many more, have left us a legacy of hope in the midst of despair, of faith forcing its way through the bedrock of fear, and of the joy of God undergirding the many vicissitudes of life. They also share their experience of the creator who meets them in the deep places of human experience and teaches them to be still in God's loving presence.

Those whose journals have come down to us did not write with publication in mind. They were simply recording their own experience and, in the process, clarifying it and discerning the presence and providence of God. We may learn a great deal about them, and about ourselves, as we read their journals, especially as we find them articulating our own unspoken questions and needs. But that was not their purpose in writing. Like us they were Christian believers attempting to live out their commitment to Christ, and to continue the faith journey in the spirit of the gospel. Like us they sometimes stumbled, sometimes doubted and sometimes came to a complete stop, wondering where God was and whether it was possible to go on. There were moments of exhilaration when their blurred vision became transformed into focused seeing by the presence of the living Lord. There were times when the ordinary became the vehicle of the holy and Christ was made known to them unexpectedly, as he was to early disciples in the breaking of bread. They shared our humanity and our questions, though they may have lived in different times and contexts. And they each wrote of their experience in journal form.

Journaling is not just for the giants of Christian history. It is a means of grace available to each one of us, a way to grow in the life of faith. Keeping a journal is not simply a recording of thoughts and events but a process by which those things take on new levels of meaning. The present moment finds its place in a wider context and, as it is written down, draws to itself the wisdom of the past while it indicates a response to the future characterized by hope. The value of journal keeping is well expressed by Edward J. Farrell: "The Journal is a putting into words the praise of God that leaps from the transparencies of life which the light of faith illumines for us."[1]

I am frequently surprised when I see color slides I

have taken projected onto a screen. There is not only a happy recalling of the places and people who were caught in a split second by the camera shutter, but a recalling of sounds, scents, the warmth of the sun or crunch of snow at my feet, the feelings of joy or poignancy. Special human relationships and moments of awe are evoked as I see again mountains, skies, oceans inviting a fresh response. Sometimes I will be stirred afresh to pray for someone now distant who was once an important part of my life. Perhaps the memories will remind me of a period of spiritual growth which was especially graced, and will invite me to deeper commitment at the present time. Possibly a scene may invoke sadness because it speaks only of loss and the need to pay attention to grief. Much the same process takes place as we begin to commit to writing our day by day experience. We record one little moment, one transparency, and we find God shining through. We are also reminded of many similar experiences and of how we responded on those occasions. Our prayer may then be for help and guidance, or it may be that praise and thanksgiving are evoked. Sometimes we will need to ask God for healing and forgiveness and the courage to go on.

The journal helps us take the road inward and so to discover who we really are. As we write, the ambiguity of human experience with its hidden desires and impulses is revealed. Our questions increase and need to be explored, not so much to resolve them as to place them in the context of the mystery at the heart of the universe. We learn to be present in the waiting, the place of not-knowing, and to trust. Honest self-scrutiny was a characteristic of the life of Dietrich Bonhoeffer. In his ministry to the confessing church, in the decision which led him, as a pacifist, to become implicated in the plot to assassinate Hitler, and in the isolation of his cell, he allowed the painful tension of conflicting claims to be expressed. From prison he wrote:

> Who am I? They often tell me
> I stepped from my cell's confinement
> Calmly, cheerfully, firmly,
> Like a squire from his country house.
> Who am I? They often tell me
> I used to speak to my warders
> Freely and friendly and clearly
> As though it were mine to command.
> Who am I? They also tell me
> I bore the days of misfortune
> Equably, smilingly, proudly
> Like one accustomed to win.[2]

This was how others saw him, a man of faith, courage and hope, but the unseen, internal struggle was also part of his experience. Confined and cut off from friends and the church he had served with such passion he felt:

Restless and longing and sick, like a bird in a cage
Struggling for breath, as though hands were compress-
     ing my throat,
Yearning for colours, for flowers, for the voices of birds,
Thirsting for words of kindness, for neighbourliness,
Tossing in expectation of great events,
Powerlessly trembling for friends at an infinite distance,
Weary and empty at praying, at thinking, at waiting,
Faint, and ready to say farewell to it all?

Who am I? This or the other?
Am I one person today and tomorrow another?
Am I both at once? A hypocrite before others,
And before myself a contemptibly woebegone weakling?

Or is something within me still like a beaten army
Fleeing in disorder from victory already achieved?

Who am I? They mock me, these lonely questions of
   mine.
Whoever I am, Thou knowest, O God, I am thine.[3]

Like John the Baptist imprisoned by Herod, Bonhoeffer struggled with doubt, fear, and the disorientation of
incarceration. His vocation seemed to have shut him up
in a dark place where, alone with himself, the demons of
despair directed all their venom at him. The answer to
this kind of question is not found in either-or categories.
Growth in self-knowledge teaches us that we are a glorious, rag-bag collection of motivations, beliefs and insecu-
rities. At times we are people of courage with our faith
firmly rooted in God, but we are also subject to fear and
uncertainty. We wrestle inwardly with our inconsistency
and the contradictoriness of so much of life. The journal
enables us to say "Yes, I am this" while I acknowledge that
I am also "that," and in the present time the two do not
seem reconcilable. I consent to live with ambiguity and to
celebrate the wonder of God's grace which constantly
supplies me with the strength to be and to become.
   This book is written for those who are seeking God
and who are willing to allow memory, reason, imagination, faith and will to be engaged as they journal their
prayer. The exercises, suggestions and guidelines are designed to support the goal of being found and transformed
by the living God who loves us and delights in us. This
quest is serious and playful; it is full of surprises for our
creator is always making things new and filling life with
fresh meaning. Anyone who can write may take this way of
prayer and be enriched by the creative insights it offers.

How To Begin

There is no "right" way to keep a journal. I find that a looseleaf notebook is the most flexible because it enables me to make insertions and add material later as interconnecting thoughts occur. It also means that when I travel, several sheets of paper are all I need to carry and these can be added to my journal later. Other people I know prefer an attractively bound book, with either a leather or a fabric cover that looks really special. Still others are content with a spiral notebook. The important thing is to choose what appeals most to you and to make the journal special. Notes jotted on scraps of paper tend to get lost and may suggest a less than serious attempt to pursue the prayer journey through journaling.

I write in my journal most days, but because I have a tendency to create rules and structures, I give myself the freedom to spend time with my journal when I choose. There are no "oughts" about writing in it. I do find, however, that if I neglect it for several days, there is a real sense of loss. I need to write again, just as I need to pick up the telephone to call a friend I have not spoken to for some time. I begin each entry by writing the date and often include a note about where I am, especially if I am traveling. Because in my tradition the liturgical calendar is followed, I make a record of saints' days or other celebrations, and these often give rise to reflections which become part of the journal entry. For a person who is less inclined to create regular patterns of life, a personal "rule" may well be a necessary aid to writing. The word journal is derived from a Middle English word which referred to a *daily* service book, and the greatest benefit is gained by a real commitment to consistent entries.

Each person will need to find the right time for journaling. I am a "morning person" and find that the hour or so after the first cup of coffee is a perfect time for the kind of silence and reflection which gives rise to journal writing. For those who are most energized at night, my pattern will not work. A mother with young children at home may need to claim nap time for writing since this offers the only really undisturbed moments of the day. Morton Kelsey in his book *Adventure Inward* tells of the way in which he is often wakened in the night, and some very fruitful dialogue with God gets recorded in his journal during those times. It is important to take time, and perhaps to experiment a little, to discover what is the most appropriate time for you to journal.

Silence is an important preparation for journaling. Sometimes a way into silence may be through meditative music or through stretching and breathing exercises. Taking time to become centered and to be conscious of the messages our body is sending to us will help in the process of listening and awareness. It may be that I feel tired, and in the awareness of low energy I remember that yesterday was too busy and disorganized. This may be exactly the place to start journaling as I talk with God about my tendency to over-schedule and begin to explore some of the reasons for this. My prayer may then become one for wisdom to choose healthier patterns of work and relationships, and a commitment to safeguard quality time for prayerful reflection.

As soon as I settle down for prayer, distractions start to occur. I remember a phone call that has to be made, something to add to the grocery list, or a birthday card that has to be sent. I have learned to keep a notebook—not my journal—at hand, so that these things can be quickly jotted down in order that I may return to my prayer journal. Sometimes it is appropriate to pray the distractions, especially if a situation constantly inserts itself into consciousness. It may be that God is inviting me to journal a problem or relationship that is causing difficulty because I have not been willing to pay attention to the issues raised.

Some people are more able to write freely if they use a typewriter, and this will work as long as each page is added regularly to a journal notebook. Anxiety about legibility, spelling, and grammar needs to be put aside, and that may be difficult for some of us, conditioned by our education to expect bad grades if work is not "right." I recall the frustration of sitting in school next to a girl whose work was always meticulously neat and grammatically correct but rather dull. I had a very active imagination and loved writing stories but my book was always returned with much red ink indicating the unacceptability of ink blots, misspelled words and poor punctuation. It seemed unjust that no reward was offered for creativity, only for appearance, and I began to lose interest in writing. My journal is personal and need never be seen by another person, and that frees me to dispense with the old "messages" that it has to look good and be correct in order to be acceptable.

Confidentiality is also important. I keep my journal in a locked drawer to ensure that I am the only person who sees it unless I choose to share some part with a trusted friend. This means that I do not have to censor my writing, although when I am writing about individuals or situations about which my words might be hurtful if inadvertently observed, I use code names. I have added a codicil to my will about the disposal of my journals at my death, and all of this adds to a sense of security as I write.

Beginning a journal moves us into a new stage of the journey toward wholeness, integration and a deepening relationship with God. It is a deceptively simple means of grace for us. We need only to desire and decide to begin—that is the first and most significant step—and the One who calls us into life is ready to respond with ever new and transforming gifts of love.

Telling the Good News

It was not until some twenty or thirty years after the death of Jesus that Christian communities began to recognize the need for written records of his life and teaching. St. Mark wrote his gospel and others followed, each telling in his own way the good news about the resurrection of Christ and the hope this brings to the world. There is a sense in which we are engaging in this same process as we journal; we are telling the good news of the presence and power of the risen Christ in our lives and in the world. We are writing a kind of fifth gospel. Our journals will also contain stories of waiting, struggle with evil, healing events, encounters with those who support and hinder our journey, and the death and new life that occurs again and again as we allow growth to happen.

The gospel writers were engaging in a process of interpretation as they tried to find ways of saying what Christ meant to them. Often they found connections with the past and began to see the relationship between their own experience and that of God's people in history. Remembering was a very important part of interpreting the present. Journaling is a means by which we also remember, recalling our own past experience and finding our place in the procession of believers who have faced the same questions and trusted the same God. Often we pass over many significant events in our lives until we commit them to paper and begin to see how they may help us now.

Imagination and creativity get set in motion in the process of writing. Situations that look closed, relationships that seem dead, a way of seeing that has become lifeless are injected with hope and newness. The first disciples had to learn through loss that the earthly Jesus was now the risen, ascended Lord of history empowering them for ministry. This had not happened before, and it was necessary to search for new words and images to convey the gospel message. Our own journaling will likewise lead us into a fresh exploration of the creative imagination that God has planted within us, and we will also be called out to share the good news with others.

Joy was characteristic of the witness of Christian believers, but they also experienced fear, rejection, disappointment as they went out to communicate the message of Jesus. Emotion is a significant part of human experience and deserves to be affirmed and prayed. A release of emotion happens in the journal process, and the writing is part of healing past hurts and present fears. So often pain is unconsciously buried and remains an irritant until it is confronted with courage and compassion. Sometimes we may be led to seek help in the healing process as a result of having articulated the problem in our journal.

We are familiar with the movement toward self-understanding and self-actualization which is facilitated by journaling and supported by twentieth century western culture. However our goal is not the temporary relief of pain through greater self-knowledge and therapy but a deepening relationship with God. As women and men created in the divine image, we are blessed with resources beyond our imagining and the Spirit of God is at work through our minds, our hearts, our pens to bring to life the seed of creative energy within. We are inheritors and bearers of the good news that Christ is risen, and we share the joy of those who received the message before us.

Journaling with Scripture

The Old Testament book of Jeremiah, in its present form, reads somewhat like a journal. It is a collection of prose and poetry in which the prophet shares with amazing candor his struggles with God, the nation and himself. It contains accounts of historical events, sermons, striking symbolic actions, prayers and long inner wrestling with the God who appears to have trapped Jeremiah in a vocation he did not seek. More than any other prophet, Jeremiah reveals his inner journey, and in him I find much of my own experience reflected and affirmed. Jeremiah will be the starting point of the process of journaling with scripture as we look at some of the themes that emerge from his writing. This is not a verse-by-verse commentary on the prophetic book, but an attempt to identify and connect with significant images and metaphors that have their own meaning today. There is a sense in which Jeremiah's journey is timeless, for it is the human journey whose contours are the same today as we travel with men and women of faith in every age, allowing the creator God to meet us at each stage on the way.

The present book of Jeremiah concludes with a nonending. What happened to the prophet finally? Did God vindicate him? We do not know, and it is appropriate that we are left with our questions. There is a similar phenomenon in the gospels. The story is unfinished, there is more to be said, and that is good news for us. This is our story and faith, which call for expression in every generation. We are today's authors, finding ways to experience and tell the good news so that it connects deeply with the day to day living of contemporary believers. Journaling is a powerful means of telling the story for ourselves in such a way that we truly enter into it. It is one of the ways in which commitment is clarified, direction is discovered and prayer is deepened. Out of that process comes a fresh desire and power to share God's good news as we support each other on the journey.

The questions and exercises offered in this book are designed to serve as tools, and their purpose is to enable each person to build and grow in the life of faith, discerning the call of God in daily life. The process will also involve some demolishing of structures which are no longer life-giving, and rooting out weeds that choke healthy growth. In the journaling, we pray our trust and our resistance, our confidence and fear, our delight in God and our sense of aloneness. The creator God who calls walks with us and makes possible our life journey so that we become agents of fresh hope to others.

> See. I have set you this day over nations and over kingdoms, to pluck up and to break down, to destroy and to overthrow, to build and to plant (Jer 1:10).

Time To Begin

It is important to take as much time as you need with the exercises and reflections offered in this book. Sometimes a journal question will evoke a great deal of writing and will offer many rich insights that you will want to savor, enjoy and pray. Allow the Spirit of God to lead you, and let go of the inclination to rush on to the next phase. The purpose of the book is to enable each of us to sense

God's presence and to deepen the relationship we already have with the creator, not to complete an assignment!

Now take some time to sit down, relax and become still. If it is difficult to let go of other thoughts, listen to some quiet music as you breathe deeply and easily. As you become centered, imagine a river across which twelve stepping stones offer access to the opposite bank. Begin to see the stepping stones as significant moments in your life when you had some awareness of God's reality and presence. Start with early childhood, your first awareness of God, and describe in your journal each of the stepping stones and your response. As you recognize these stages on your life journey, begin to pray the feelings of gratitude, confusion, joy, anxiety, hope and other emotions that emerge.

When you are ready to go on, look again at the stepping stones and see if you can find any patterns of response that become clear. Is there always a gladness or wariness when you sense that God is near? Do you respond with willing obedience or resistance? Remember that you are not sitting in judgment on yourself but seeking to grow in awareness of your relationship with God. Be aware of your feelings *now* as you continue the journey of faith and write a brief prayer that expresses your desire at this time.

1

A Nation in Crisis: Jeremiah in His Time

*J*eremiah lived in a time of political turmoil when the world as he knew it was poised on the edge of catastrophe. His life, and therefore his writing, was deeply affected by what he saw. His faith in God was tested as he experienced change, destruction and exile in the nation and he knew deep personal anguish as he tried to make sense of his vocation. Some understanding of the context in which he ministered will enable us, who also live in a rapidly changing and potentially destructive world, to make our own connections with his story.

Jeremiah frequently questioned God. Sometimes he felt abandoned, and often the problems facing the world seemed too overwhelming for him. He spoke with zeal on moral issues and called the people of the covenant back to faithful living. Much of the time he met with little apparent success. Before moving on to the historical background of his life, we pause to reflect on the turmoil of our time that nightly fills our TV screens. Drug related violence, homelessness, consumerism assault us; war, hunger and need exist in a global village where inequity prevails. Where is God? Can our small efforts make a difference? How do we go on believing and working for justice and peace? These questions, and many more, ask to be allowed into our consciousness not just so that we find "answers" but in order to help us pray the confusion and doubt.

Journal Exercise

Once again take time to enter into a quiet space and review for a few moments the stepping stones exercise. As you recall those graced times when you became aware of God, read Psalm 139:1–11 slowly and meditatively. Read the same passage again; this time imagine yourself to be the psalmist, aware of God's all-pervading presence. How do you feel about God being behind, in front and above you, laying a hand on you? Are you glad or fearful to discover God's presence in the darkness? How does this relate to your sense of the turmoil and need of the world? When you are ready, record your reflections and feelings in your journal.

The Growth of a Nation

The earliest origins of the people of Israel are found in the stories of migratory wanderings, focused especially on the patriarch Abraham. From a developed civilization in Chaldea, a movement northwest along the course of the Euphrates valley began. The biblical writers interpret this as a faith journey undertaken in response to divine initiative and accompanied by a promise:

By faith Abraham obeyed when he was called to go out to a place which he was to receive as an inheritance; and he went out, not knowing where he was to go. By faith he sojourned in the land of promise, as in a foreign land, living in tents with

> Isaac and Jacob, heirs with him of the same prom-
> ise (Heb 11:8-9).

A further stage in the journey took place when those
Semites who had become slaves in Egypt were led out of
captivity by Moses. The exodus became a focal point in
history, and a symbol of hope for oppressed people in
every age. God's people went into the desert where,
through hunger, weariness and conflict with enemies,
they learned the cost of such a pilgrimage. It was a going
out, a letting go of the past, in order to find new life and a
future conceived in promise.

Over many centuries, various tribal groups settled in
what we now call Israel, some of them entering under the
leadership of Joshua after he defeated the fortified city of
Jericho. A loose confederation of tribes was formed, and
different combinations of them came together to do battle
with other would-be settlers. The Philistines in particular
appear often in the biblical narratives as a strong, well-
defended force with which the tribes had to contend. As
time went on, some of the tribes thought it appropriate to
elect a king to give prestige to their cause. The young,
charismatic warrior Saul was chosen—a choice which was
perceived in some of the tradition as an unmitigated disaster since it represented rejection of Yahweh, and else-
where as the fulfillment of divine purpose. During the
tenth century B.C. the descendants of those who left
Egypt, together with other groups who joined them, were
welded into a nation. The unlikely choice of David as king
in place of Saul proved to be a cohesive factor, and under
his leadership the kingdom grew geographically. The former Jebusite stronghold, Jerusalem, was captured and
became the capital of the new nation. A major building

program was begun. This included the construction of a royal palace in Jerusalem and plans for the building of the temple, later to become the center of Israel's worship. Trade negotiations with other nations increased the importance of Israel, not least because she now controlled one of the major trade routes in the ancient Near East.

David died in 961 B.C. and was succeeded by his son Solomon. The new king not only continued the vigorous construction work begun during his father's reign, but he also established a huge smelting works in Ezion Geber and imported substantial numbers of horses and chariots from Egypt. These were stabled at Megeido on the plane of Esdraelon. A considerable labor force was needed for all the new industry, and to provide it Solomon introduced conscription. Most of the forced labor came from the tribes in the north, and the smoldering unrest which had developed in David's day was now fanned into flame. The temple was completed and dedicated with great ceremony to the worship of Yahweh, God of Israel, but alongside the rejoicing, civil unrest grew. With the succession of Rehoboam, Solomon's son, it erupted. The northern tribes, under the leadership of Jeroboam, came to the new king asking for an easing of the harsh conditions under which the laborers worked. Rehoboam consulted his younger counselors, rejecting the advice of the men who had previously served in that capacity, and refused the request. Instead of an easing of conditions, he threatened to increase pressure. A military coup followed and the kingdom was divided. Jeroboam became king over the northern territory of Israel, and Rehoboam retained the smaller, southern section now called Judah.

During the course of the next two hundred years hostility and intrigue characterized relations between Israel and Judah and their respective allies. Occasional interludes of rapprochement were short-lived, and a sense of superiority prevailed in the south where the temple provided a focus for national identity. As a means of establishing political and religious independence in the north, two shrines were built, strategically placed near the northern and southern borders. Omri, who succeeded Jeroboam I, established his capital—almost a replica of Jerusalem—at Samaria. This centrally located and highly fortified city seemed almost impregnable to invading armies. Internal struggles between the two countries continued, sometimes blinding them to the rise of super-powers close to their borders. In the south, where the Davidic line had been established, the monarchy and the temple in Jerusalem represented some stability. In Israel, however, one king followed another in rapid and bloody succession. Syria was a force to be reckoned with on her northern borders, but gradually Assyria gained the ascendancy, moving ever closer to Israel. When Damascus, the Syrian capital, fell to the might of the invading Assyrian armies, it was only a matter of time until Israel also capitulated.

In 722 B.C., amidst scenes of terrible violence, destruction, torture and desecration, Israel came to an end. The biblical writers whose work has been preserved for us record events largely from a southern perspective. They viewed the devastation as Yahweh's judgment on an evil nation which had rejected the covenant. Compromise with foreign worship, and rejection of religious and political unity centered in the Davidic monarchy, were regarded as the cause of divine punishment. Assyria moved further south and attacked Jerusalem, but her armies were miraculously driven back. This was perceived as a sign of Yahweh's approval of Judah, a clear indication that God was on her side. So much significance was attached to this victory that there grew up a belief in the inviolability of

Jerusalem. This was Yahweh's city, the center of the whole earth, and clearly nothing could destroy it or the temple. Such confidence led to complacency. In the north the prophetic voice had been frequently raised against kings and political leaders, while southern prophets, like Isaiah of Jerusalem, worked in close cooperation with the monarchy. This made Jeremiah's message all the more distasteful since it ran counter to tradition.

Geographical location also played a major role in the relative peacefulness of Judah. Away from the major trade routes, with its capital heavily fortified and at an elevation of thirteen thousand feet, it was not an inviting target for attack. Israel had provided a buffer against Assyrian aggression, and the initial, unsuccessful, attempt to take Jerusalem following the fall of the northern kingdom was followed by a period of internal struggle in Assyria. Not until the great Babylonian empire gained ascendancy did the most serious threat to Judah's existence arise. It was against the background of the ominous "foe from the north" that many of Jeremiah's warnings were uttered. The prophet's ministry spanned a period of at least forty years, 627–587 B.C., but most of the book which bears his name focuses on the latter part of his life. When the fate he had forecast finally befell his people in 587 B.C., he shared the experience. The intelligentsia and artisans were deported in large numbers to Babylon, leaving behind peasant farmers and the poor of the land. With the loss of roots, a homeland and the temple, it is little wonder that the exiles turned to lament:

By the waters of Babylon we sat down and wept,
    when we remembered you, O Zion.
As for our harps, we hung them up
    on the trees in the midst of that land.

> For those who led us away captive asked us for a song,
>   and our oppressors called for mirth.
> "Sing to us one of the songs of Zion."
> How shall we sing the Lord's song
>   upon an alien soil? (Ps 137:1–4)

It was then that Jeremiah began a ministry of encouragement and hope, writing to the exiles in Babylon, encouraging them to build houses and raise families. Like Jacob fleeing many years before from home, they made the discovery:

> Surely the Lord is in this place, and I did not know it (Gen 28:16).

The God whose presence graced the temple in Jerusalem was no less present in the place of suffering and exile. Out of apparent disaster a people was reborn, and given a new heart, a deeper community and hope. Jeremiah inspired them, in the extremes of their despair, with fresh energy and confidence for the future by proclaiming the word of Yahweh:

> I will bring them back to this place, and I will make them dwell in safety. And they shall be my people, and I will be their God. I will give them one heart and one way, that they may fear me forever, for their own good and also the good of their children after them. I will make with them an everlasting covenant, that I will not turn away from doing good to them (Jer 32:37–40).

Jeremiah did not live to see the return of the exiles to their own native land, but his words lived on to encourage them in their waiting, and they still have a ring of truth for today's pilgrims and exiles who seek to find God in an unstable and fearful world.

Reflection

What signs of hope do you see in the church and the world? Record your reflections and ask how you can be a source of encouragement to those who may be despondent.

2

Call and Conflict

See, I have set you this day over nations and over kingdoms, to pluck up and to break down, to destroy and to overthrow, to build and to plant (Jer 1:10).

*T*here are decisive moments in human experience when the call of God is heard and heeded. For some the word comes with blinding clarity so that, like Paul, former ways of seeing are shattered as fresh vision creates energy for action. Others hear in the stillness of the night an unidentified voice that calls persistently until there is response, as in 1 Samuel 3. On a mountain after earthquake, wind and fire shake the foundations, a quiet voice is heard in the silence and a prophet returns to his task, as related in 1 Kings 19:11-13. In the craggy wilderness of Tekoa, a shepherd listens to God speak in tones which evoke terror like the marauding lion, and Amos bursts upon the scene, proclaiming judgment on a society bent on oppression, injustice and violence. Esther, in fear of her life, allows the inner call to be heard and intercedes on behalf of her nation, exposing the insane antisemitism of Haman, and bringing new hope to her people. These, and all God's people throughout time, come to that moment of response, and the answer they give transforms history.

The moment of decision, however, usually has a history of its own. For most of us God's call is heard and repeated many times, inviting our response in ever clearer and deeper ways. This was the case with Jeremiah "to whom the word of the Lord came in the days of Josiah" (Jer 1:2), for the text goes on to say: "It came also in the days of Jehoiakim the son of Josiah, king of Judah, and until the end of the eleventh year of Zedekiah, the son of Josiah king of Judah, until the captivity of Jerusalem in the fifth month" (Jer 1:3). Jeremiah was listening to the voice of God for forty years, from 627 to 587 B.C., and he was engaging in a struggle with his resistance to a vocation he did not choose. That struggle is enshrined in the account of his call told in the opening chapter.

No doubt Jeremiah thought that he had identified his place in the scheme of things. He was a descendant of the priest Abiathar whom Solomon banished to Anathoth for his support of Adonijah who tried to usurp the throne (1 Kgs 2:26–27). There is no clear statement that Jeremiah's father Hilkiah actually functioned as a priest, though he may well have instructed the people in the law and presided over sacrifices in the village, a practice that would be changed by Josiah's reforms. Be that as it may, Jeremiah had a deep feeling for Israel's ancient traditions, and he twice expressed concern for the shrine at Shiloh, twenty miles north of Anathoth (Jer 7:14; 26:6). Although his oracles and the outlook embodied in the book are usually in contrast to priestly tradition, his background was more rooted there than in prophetic ways of thinking. Hence he found himself resisting the call of God.

Reading Reflection

Read reflectively Jeremiah 1:1–10. As you do so, allow yourself to be drawn into the experience of the prophet, and be aware of any connections you feel between his responses and your own relating to God. In your journal record your reactions, mentioning any specific events that come to mind. Does this reflection relate at all to any of your "stepping stones"?

Jeremiah's Call

His appointment as a prophet, Jeremiah learns, preceded his conception, for it was in the mind of God long before his birth. Three very significant words are used in the opening statement in which God begins a dialogue with Jeremiah: "Before I formed you in the womb I *knew* you and before you were born I *consecrated* you; I *appointed* you a prophet to the nations" (Jer 1:5). In Hebrew idiom to speak of knowing meant something deeper than intellectual understanding; it implied intimacy and commitment. In Genesis 4:1 it is used of intercourse between a man and a woman, and the eighth century prophets used the term to depict the deep intimacy between Yahweh and the covenant people—an intimacy they often desecrated through whoredom (cf. Am 3:2; Hos 4:1). There is in Jeremiah's call a reassuring statement of the profound relationship already existing between God and the prophet-to-be, and this reassurance would be much needed in those moments when Jeremiah felt abandoned and alone.

The second verb emphasizes another aspect of commitment, the setting apart of a person or object for a very specific, holy purpose. Jeremiah was to be no longer his own person but God's, consecrated to the prophetic task for which he had been conceived. The word used for "appoint" is also found in Genesis 1:17; 17:5, Exodus 7:1, and Isaiah 49:6 and indicates a special and particular respon-

sibility. The stars are appointed to give light, Abraham to
be forebear of a great nation, Moses to liberate the Israelites, God's servant Israel to shed light on the nations,
Jeremiah to be a prophetic voice in Judah during a period
of political unrest and religious complacency. Jeremiah is
known, consecrated and appointed by God for a vocation
he did not desire, and so begins the dialogue in which he
tries to escape the divine summons.

"Ah, Lord God! Behold, I do not know how to speak,
for I am only a youth" (Jer 1:6). The response was brief
and, no doubt, true. Faced with the call to speak to nations
on behalf of God, Jeremiah is aware only of his inexperi-
ence and lack of training in the skills of oratory. The great
super-powers Assyria, Babylon and Egypt were constantly
making their oppressive presence felt on Judah's borders.
Smaller nations like Edom, Moab, Philistia and Ammon—
nations against whom Amos railed more than a century
earlier—were still enemies to be reckoned with. How
could someone as inexperienced and inarticulate as Jeremiah speak intelligently of the political, social and spiritual dangers endemic in his society?

The sense of inadequacy for the task and the attempt
to escape its obligations appear frequently in stories of
call to ministry. Moses experienced the numinous presence of God in a burning bush and heard in that encounter
a call to be liberator of his people. He too expressed inadequacy: "Who am I that I should go to Pharaoh and
bring the sons of Israel out of Egypt?" (Ex 3:11). In reply
God promises the divine presence; I AM of the theophany
will liberate the people through the agency of Moses. Still
excuses are offered—"They will not believe me or listen
to my voice"—and God responds with miraculous signs.
Moses has not yet done with resistance, saying "My Lord, I
am not eloquent," and God replies: "I will be with your

mouth" (Ex 4:13). Finally Moses reaches the bottom line: "My Lord, send, I pray, some other person!" God is angry but does not withdraw the call, though Aaron is sent as a support for Moses.

The call of God is not aborted by excuses. The dialogue with Jeremiah continues with a repetition of the obligation to go and the reassurance that God's presence will be with him. "Do not say, 'I am only a youth'; for to all to whom I send you, you shall go, and whatever I command you, you shall speak. Be not afraid of them, for I am with you to deliver you, says the Lord" (Jer 1:7-8). There is an imperiousness about God's summons, and our inadequacy and lack of experience become the occasion of God's enabling grace. God did not promise the absence of conflict but the capacity to go on with the assigned task. Then Jeremiah is touched in the place of his greatest need. He had declared the inadequacy of his speech, and like Isaiah who owned the unworthiness of his lips to speak for a holy God (Is 6), Jeremiah is touched on the mouth. Again his task is spelled out, and the rest of the book illuminates the ways in which Jeremiah fulfilled the divine assignment to "pluck up and to break down, to destroy and to overthrow, to build and to plant" (Jer 1:10). The prophet would proclaim oracles concerning the destruction and restoration of kingdoms. He would challenge God's people, predicting the destruction of the temple, their center of worship, and later encourage with hope those who were exiled in Babylon. He would shatter a pottery vase to lend force to God's word of doom, and bury a loincloth in a field, bought at the moment of greatest economic disaster, as a sign of restoration and return. His message matched the moment and was faithful to the ambiguity of his call.

The call of God invites resistance because it plunges

us into change and vulnerability, and we have a basic urge to avoid both. It makes us choose between options and that means letting go of some desires. "Leaving the options open" can become a weak excuse for the refusal to relinquish a particular way of perceiving God, the world, or our call, so that our voice is not heard. Resistance is a reality in most of our living and not only when our wills come into conflict with God's. It is part of normal, healthy human experience, and if there is an absence of resistance to God, we might do well to ask ourselves whether we are pursuing our vocation with any seriousness. Resistance is a sign of life, engagement, and growth.

Jeremiah was invited to be intimate with the creator God, and like most of us he desired and dreaded intimacy. We long to know God, to fulfill God's purpose, to experience abundant life in communion with the One who made us. Then when fresh opportunities are given to say "yes" to the divine will, we become like Jonah, ready to take a ship in the opposite direction! Francis Thompson expresses so well the desire to escape, and the attempt to run from God's persistent call, in the poem "The Hound of Heaven":

I fled him down the nights and down the days,
I fled him down the arches of the years;
I fled him down the labyrinthine ways
Of my own mind; and in the midst of tears
I hid from him; and under running laughter
    Up vistaed hopes I sped
    and shot, precipitated
Adown Titanic glooms of chasmed fears.
From those strong feet that followed, followed after.
    But with unhurrying chase
    And unperturbed pace

Deliberate speed, majestic instancy,
   They beat—and a Voice beat
   More instant than the feet—
"All things betray thee, who betrayest me."[1]

God always catches up with us. When we stop, in our quiet moments, we face our resistance and enter into dialogue with the divine Word. And we are truly inventive when it comes to excuses! Often we sound so convincing that we begin to believe in our feeble attempts to escape the cost of obedience. A young nurse who had experienced a long sense of call to offer herself for missionary service overseas became so troubled by her lack of peace that she confided in her pastor. She told him of the sense of fulfillment she derived from her chosen profession, of the patients she cared for in the hospital where she worked, and of her commitment to sharing her faith with colleagues. She also spoke of her parents, both healthy and mobile but aging, and needing her. At the same time she owned that the sense of call to work in the third world invaded her prayer time, and left her feeling unhappy and anxious. Her reasons for not responding to that inner voice, though plausible, did not ring true, but the pastor was wise enough not to say so. Instead he opened the Bible to Acts 10, the story of Peter's visionary experience on the rooftop at Caesarea, and pointed to verse 14. God had told Peter to eat of animals traditionally regarded as unclean, a prefiguring of events soon to take place when he entered the home of "unclean" Gentiles, and Peter said "No, Lord." "That is something you cannot say to God. It either has to be 'No' or 'Lord,'" said the pastor, and left her with the scriptures. God is insistent but does not coerce us, though we need to recognize what we are doing as we respond. Procrastination is a way of saying no. Sometime later the pastor and nurse prayed, laughed and wept together as she held a tear-stained Bible in which the word "No" had been erased.

Often the reasons we offer for not responding to God's call have more than a grain of truth in them. We *are* inadequate, we *do* feel fearful as we remember past failures, we *are* poor speakers, organizers, and scholars, and people need us where we are now. But God does not ask for proficiency, only for obedience, a rather old-fashioned word in a society in which self-fulfillment is presented as ultimate. St. Paul writes of his "thorn in the flesh" and of the repeated requests he made to God to remove it. God did not take away this source of irritation, but he assured the apostle: "My grace is sufficient for you, for my power is made perfect in weakness" (2 Cor 12:9). In the extreme of our need and sense of inadequacy, and usually only in that place, we learn to rely on God who is our only secure source of power. It is on God's authority that we speak and act, though we may appear to fail or look like fools in the eyes of our contemporaries. Jeremiah was an object of scorn on many occasions. But the God who knows, consecrates and appoints us to be agents of hope and reconciliation in a broken world also enables us.

Jeremiah's lips were touched by God when he owned his inability to speak clearly. Throughout the gospels the touch of Jesus brought healing and strength to those who were sick, weak and afraid. God's touch of compassion is known in our lives also as we bring into the divine presence, and into our consciousness, the fears that keep us from saying yes. Often the touch comes through the gentle support and understanding of those whose honesty we value. Sometimes in moments of solitude, when we find the courage to stay with our aloneness and fear, we feel the hand of God upon us. In our penitential coming to the creator whom we have denied and wounded, we are healed and empowered. There is good reason why the sacrament of reconciliation (confession) is frequently concluded by the priest laying hands on the penitent's head at the words of absolution. We need tangible ways of experiencing the touch of love, and God chooses often to touch us through others who are the vehicles of divine compassion. So we receive forgiveness, the healing hand of God in our lives, and the opening up of the possibility of a yes response as we begin again to hear the call.

Jeremiah struggled, like us, with desire and resistance to the divine will. In the dialogue which occurs at the beginning of this collection of writings, he opens up a way for us to enter into conversation with God who calls. We connect with his experience, but the response we make is our own, pertinent to our life situation at this moment. And the One who calls so imperiously waits to sustain, empower and send us out to incarnate God's word.

Journal Exercises

One helpful method of journaling is to write in dialogue form. After the usual settling down and becoming quiet, begin to articulate silently the questions you wish to ask God and begin to listen to God's word to you. When you are ready, allow the response to come from deep within yourself. This may have a sense of artificiality about it to begin with, but the very act of committing to writing the conversation between yourself and God brings clarity and encouragement. I am constantly surprised as I do this that God is so much less punitive than I often imagine, and

frequently draws me into joyful play and celebration. The
following questions suggest a way to begin this process:

1. What is God calling you to become or do at this time?
   Begin your response by allowing God to speak:
   *"Before I formed you in the womb I knew you, and
   before you were born I consecrated you; I appointed
   you . . ."*

2. Write your answer to this call, beginning as Jeremiah
   did: *"Then I said, 'Ah, Lord God! Behold I . . .'"*

3. Continue this journal dialogue with God as long as you
   need to. You may find that there is a need to pick up the
   conversation again in days to come as more questions
   or insights arise.

3

Continuity and Discontinuity

I went down to the potter's house, and there he
was working at his wheel. And the vessel he was
making was spoiled in the potter's hand, and he
reworked it as it seemed good to the potter to do.
Then the word of the Lord came to me: "O house
of Israel, can I not do with you as this potter has
done? says the Lord. Behold, like the clay in the
potter's hand, so are you in my hand, O house of
Israel" (Jer 18:3-6).

*T*he destiny of Jerusalem, holy and beloved city, is central to the message of Jeremiah. His call made clear the
nature of his prophetic ministry, "to pluck up and break
down, to destroy and overthrow, to build and to plant."
No wonder he resisted such a vocation, for it meant placing himself over against the ideology, theology and national pride of his day. Uncompromisingly he announced the
doom of Jerusalem and the end of an era. Shockingly he
spoke of Yahweh's alliance with the Babylonian king, and
of the inevitability of exile. Tenaciously he clung to the
second part of his call "to build and to plant" even when
faith was tested to the limit. He kept alive hope for a new
Israel, but never forgot that the old must first die.

The story of God's people recorded in the scriptures is our story. It tells of faith and new beginnings, of overcoming odds and of moving toward the realization of our destiny as those created in the divine image to receive and be blessing. It is a story of victory, celebration, and thanksgiving. But the story also takes us through doubt and darkness. There are times of sinking, stopping, or being stuck in a place from which there seems to be no escape. The loss of old ways of traveling and relating causes anxiety, even despair and a resentful questioning of the very existence of God in whom we thought we believed. Past experience needs constantly to be reinterpreted if we are to make sense of the present. And often much cherished idols have to be destroyed before new hope can become reality. We too experience ourselves caught in the tension between continuity and discontinuity, growth and stagnation, the old and the new. The plucking up, breaking down, destroying and overthrowing is a necessary prelude to the building and planting which means new life. Jeremiah speaks not only to those who lived through the turbulence of defeat and exile in the sixth century B.C., but to all who consent to the process of pilgrimage. He speaks to us. The spoiled vase is reworkable, and the old clay can be molded into a new creation.

Journal Exercises

Take a few minutes to return to the story of the potter recorded at the beginning of this chapter. In it Jeremiah sees possibilities for change and the reworking of what seems to be misshapen and spoiled. Be aware of the breath entering your lungs, remembering that God's Spirit is breath moving in all created things. As you exhale, let go of tension, anxiety, distracting thoughts. If distractions persist, image them as clouds, appearing and then drifting away as you become more quiet within. Often we try to find images of God, asking ourselves: "How do I see God at this time?" Now consider the question, "How does God see me?" Take time to imagine how you appear to the One who created you. How do you look? Where are you located? Are you standing, sitting, moving? Are there others with you? Imagine a conversation in which God tells you how you are perceived, and when you have listened, begin a dialogue in response. When you are ready, begin to describe the experience in your journal. You may wish to write this as a continued dialogue, to describe the feelings, or even to draw the image (remember that this is *your* journal, and no one will need to comment on your expertise as an artist).

Now ask yourself if there are things which need to come to an end before you can take the next step on your journey. Journal with the need for "plucking up and breaking down" and be practical about how this can take place. What are the essential things which must remain and provide continuity in your experience? How will you make sure that these are protected?

Two Visions

Two visionary experiences are recorded immediately following Jeremiah's call, the first underscoring God's commitment to fulfill and the second illuminating its grim inexorability. The word of the Lord came to Jeremiah, saying: "Jeremiah, what do you see?" (Jer 1:11). Hearing and seeing are closely linked in prophetic understanding. Prophets are not, in the biblical sense, those who have

magical power to foretell future events. Rather they are
people who give themselves attentively to present reality.
They hear God in the midst of life, and in this way come to
fresh perceptions of the way things are. Prophets are mys-
tics insofar as attentiveness to the present, together with a
blending of intellect and intuition, enables them to envision the future. Jeremiah's images are taken from simple,
natural, homey things which become vehicles of God's
truth. "I see a rod of almond," Jeremiah tells God, and
hears in response, "You have seen well, for I am watching
over my word to perform it."

Even today Anathoth is renowned for its almond trees.
They were the first to blossom in the spring, and the closely related Hebrew words for watch and almond make this
an apt image of being awake. The almond rod speaks of
God's watchfulness over events, and is a reassurance that
Jeremiah's unpalatable message will come to pass. There
also seems to be a "waking up" in the prophet himself as
he begins to find fresh insights through familiar things.

All genuine education is a waking up to reality and
truth, a growing awareness of what is not necessarily self-
evident without attention. Prophets are true educators,
though not in the sense in which we often define education today. Too often the innate curiosity, wisdom and
creativity of children is stifled by the attempt to fill them
with information and facts, presented as essential for success. The pupil who "dreams" in class is brought sharply
back to the task in hand, and when he or she becomes
absorbed in some fantasy with earth, water or growing
things, the mind is turned to more important "facts." Util-
itarianism becomes the enemy of creativity. The prophets
know better. They illuminate the world around us because God's light is made manifest through them. They

listen, they see, and they speak a truth which comes not from the post-enlightenment, rational volumes that fill our bookshelves, but from the depths of a being in touch with the mystery at the heart of the universe.

Jeremiah's first vision is about waking up. All our beginnings spring from an awakening to fresh insight and new ways of envisioning reality. Hildegard of Bingen, the twelfth century German mystic, suffered a prolonged period of illness and depression. Self-doubt, fear, and a sense of impotence in the conflict she experienced with the church and religious authorities left her debilitated and weak. The moment she let go of these things, of what Matthew Fox, her biographer, calls the "I can't" syndrome,[1] a new way of living opened up for her. She described it as "waking up," and in the illumination she painted depicting the experience, she compares it to the day of Pentecost. Then she says to her reader:

> O human being, why do you sleep? Why do you
> have no taste for the good works which sound in
> God's ears like a symphony? Why do you not
> search out the house of your heart?[2]

Waking up to what is there lies at the heart of the prophetic and mystical expression of truth, and Hildegard reminds us that we awaken to justice and compassion—to the prophetic dimension of ourselves. The awakening is not to some world-forgetting ecstasy, but to an active participation in the purposes of God which inevitably involve judgment. Like Jeremiah, like Hildegard, we are called to the task of justice-making as we awaken to the pain of a society at odds with the creator. In eastern tradition sin is sometimes defined as being asleep! God, who watches over the word of judgment to perform it, needs our participation in the healing process, and that means waking from the sinful sleep of apathy.

Jeremiah was not selective about those he challenged to wake up to the reality of God's judgment and the end of an era. Complacency was so deeply embedded in his society that shock tactics were often necessary to reinforce his message. Other prophets were supporters of the status quo and blind to the moral, spiritual and political danger threatening the nation. They, along with priest and scribe, are accused of lying, rejecting God's word, greed, injustice, falsehood, and of proclaiming "Peace, peace, when there is no peace" (Jer 8:8-13). In another oracle (Jer 23:9-22) they are described as adulterers set on an evil course, ungodly men treading slippery paths in the darkness, against whom the wrath of Yahweh will break forth. To the people Jeremiah says:

> Do not listen to the words of the prophets who prophesy to you, filling you with vain hopes; they speak visions of their own minds, not from the mouth of the Lord. They say continually to those who despise the word of the Lord, "It shall be well with you"; and to everyone who stubbornly follows his own heart, they say, "No evil shall come upon you" (Jer 23:16-17).

This public challenge, though unheeded, generated much hostility against Jeremiah. It brought him into direct conflict with Hananiah, the prophet from Gibeon, whose name means "Yahweh has been gracious" and whose message was one of continuing protection by God. In chapter 27 God tells Jeremiah to make a yoke and to wear it as a symbol of the servitude Judah would soon experience under the Babylonians. The following chapter describes an encounter with Hananiah in the temple, his prediction of an end to Babylonian oppression, and the breaking of Jeremiah's yoke. Jeremiah in turn predicts the end of Hananiah—he died later that year—and God's inevitable judgement: "You have broken wooden bars, but I will make in their place bars of iron" (Jer 28:13).

Kings did not escape Jeremiah's word of judgement. Chapter 36 describes the writing of a scroll containing Jeremiah's message, which Baruch his scribe then took to the temple (from which Jeremiah was now barred). After reading the scroll, the princes and other dignitaries took it to King Johoiakim, who systematically sliced off each section as it was read, tossing it piece by piece into a brazier. Jeremiah and Baruch went into hiding to escape custody, and the scroll was rewritten. Later King Zedekiah sent for Jeremiah, after the prophet had been seized and unjustly incarcerated. Though his discomfort may well have tempted him to modify the message, Jeremiah resolutely repeated his prophecy of Babylonian success against Judah. His appeal to Zedekiah led to some easing of conditions, for he was transferred from the prison to the court of the guard and provided with a loaf of bread daily until supplies ran out.

Prophets, kings and his own close relatives heard the message and hated the bearer of such somber news. Jeremiah 11:21-23 offers a reassurance by Yahweh that those from Anathoth who wanted to kill Jeremiah would not succeed in their schemes, which suggests that Jeremiah prophesied there. The reaction of people in Nazareth to the preaching of Jesus is remarkably similar (Lk 4:16-30). Those who inhabit the place of tradition are acutely embarrassed by a judgment, in which they want no part, announced by one who has gone forth from their midst. All are content with the continuity of things as they are. None is ready for change, or for the discontinuity which requires loss and a restructuring of the future.

The first vision of the almond tree taught Jeremiah that God was awake and enabled the prophet himself to see and speak with alertness. The second brief visionary experience occurred as he watched a cooking pot boiling over (Jer 1:13-19). In all probability he was seeing someone's evening meal on the fire, but the bubbling liquid became the symbol of the "foe from the north" spilling over and flowing relentlessly on. The devastating impact of Jeremiah's pronouncement of judgment came because, far from seeing Babylonian captivity as an outcome of expansionism, he named it as God's will for both Judah and Babylon (cf. 17:4; 19:15; 21:4-7; 25:9; 27:6). The enemies of the covenant community are instruments of God's will; they too serve ultimate divine purposes. It is no longer possible to identify the people of God in the narrow terms most would prefer. They must see themselves in broader perspective and let go of the idolatry of nationalism.

Discontinuity is about letting go. We have a strong urge to cling to what we know even when we sense that our attachment is often to destructive ways of living and thinking. Who will I be if I change this attitude, leave that relationship, engage in some prophetic action which invites rejection? What will become of me if I refuse to be identified with cultural and religious norms and open my eyes to God's presence in other peoples and structures? Dare I leave apathy behind, say no to the victim mentality, or to injustice and false peace in my own context? Continuity is discovered in the real essence of who we are which emerges from the ashes of grief and loss after we have consented to wake up. We have a choice. The phoenix, or the phantoms described by Daniel Berrigan in his poem visualizing those on the terrace of sloth in Dante's Purgatorio, can become symbols of where we are on our pilgrimage:

Weary in limb and mind
              toward midnight we dozed
  a gibbous moon   made the stars scarce
        suddenly   a throng
broke silence
    eerie footfalls   ululations
          My hair stood up
A ghostly cavalcade
         A marathon of thin boned dead
   hurried past   like wind driven leaves
their voices
          ghostly bells   echoes of passage

       Fainter than day's solid images
    between dream and waking
   they came   passed like shadows   vanished

   I saw
hands of scholar   boneless as ribbons
    Saw   faces of monks   whose boredom
    death lifted like death masks
Now they ran   eager   on the spoor of life

      I saw
those who yawned   years away
        in   ivory towers
   fixated in airy speculation
  They pressed forward urgently
Their eyes hot as rabbi Christ
    after the wine of life

The dead? I marveled   These are the dead?
     these swift paced spirits   alight   alert at midnight
               while the living
          drift   slow of pulse
               in heady or horrid dream

               I heard half heard them
     ghostly bells   vocables of birds
               a phrase   a word

     Mary who hastened   into hill country—
and   Michael of the swift sword—
     again—You saints   your time made good—
               They were gone   My eyes
          closed round them   my arms
gathered them in like birds or bells
               or ghosts of these
               in dream[3]

     We are "called" people, and that means we are set
apart from the prevailing climate of thought and action
which gives autonomy supreme value. Like prophets we
become counter-cultural by responding to this call for, as
Walter Brueggeman says so succinctly:

     The ideology of our time is to propose that one
     can live "an uncalled life," one not referred to
     any purpose beyond one's self. . . . Autonomy is
     the predictable ground for resisting the truth of
     a call from outside self.[4]

There are subtle idolatries waiting to "catch" us because
they sound and feel like a call. A consuming passion for
one moral issue, which refuses to envision compassionate

alternatives, may be pursued with crusading zeal and willful blindness. Dogma may be rigidly promulgated without attention to praxis because any deviation threatens the end of tightly bound power structures. Evil and warmongering may be located in ideological enemies so that it is imperative to maintain an ever increasing arsenal to preserve purity and national supremacy—all of this, without any reference to God the creator of everything that is, who requires justice, mercy and compassion to all. These are both ancient and modern idolatries, masquerading as a call, but contributing to the destruction of God's people. It is against such cultural, political and ecclesiastical pride that we are called to take a stand.

Journal Questions

1. Are there issues about which God is calling you to wake up and take action? Consider the prophetic nature of your journey in personal life, the church, the world.

2. The boiling pot image enabled Jeremiah to name the enemy. What "enemies" threaten your sense of security and well-being? How do you protect yourself? Where is God in this process? Remember that naming the enemies robs them of their power.

3. Write a summary paragraph identifying what must continue and be discontinued in your life and how you intend to move forward.

4

The Messenger and
the Message

My anguish, my anguish! I writhe in pain!
　　Oh, the walls of my heart!
My heart is beating wildly;
　　I cannot keep silent;
for I hear the sound of the trumpet
　　the alarm of war.
Disaster follows hard on disaster,
　　the whole land is laid waste.
Suddenly my tents are destroyed,
　　my curtains in a moment (Jer 4:19-20).

*M*essenger and message are inextricably bound together in the book of Jeremiah. The prophet is no slick evangelist whose smooth certainty of God's approval brings him personal followers. Rather he participates in the word of judgment; he experiences God's distance from the covenant people, and he feels the anguish of abandonment and disaster. Jeremiah finds God in precarious places when faith is tested to the limit, and he refuses a simplistic view of religion. He did not attract many disciples and had no need for a Swiss bank account! Apart from the faithful scribe Baruch, who was with him in some of the worst suffering, Jeremiah was largely alone. But the integrity of this man, and the authority of his words, bear witness to an enduring faith in the God of history.

The experience of disorientation, of muddle and mis-understanding, forms a substantial part of human life. It is often tempting to think that, because difficult and incomprehensible things are happening to us, we must somehow have got off track. If only we had got the formula right, none of this would have happened and we would still be enjoying uninterrupted blessings—the joy of God's presence. Jeremiah offers us encouragement as he acknowledges the messiness of life but refuses to abandon the God who he sometimes feels has abandoned him. He clearly does not like confusion, opposition, and loss of human friendship, and sometimes he complains bitterly that this is the cost of his vocation. At the same time he refuses the illusion that to be God's person is to be free of conflict.

Some years ago a layman, speaking at a "Faith Alive" weekend in my parish, told of the change in his life since he came to Christ. His marriage, which had been on the brink of disaster, was now healed; an alienated child was reconciled; his business was prospering. In every way Christ had made him a success. It was a passionate, moving testimony, but as I listened, questions formed. Suppose, after his conversion experience, there had been no reconciliation with his wife and the child had not come home? Suppose his business failed and he had filed for bankruptcy? I rejoiced with him in this new faith, but wondered if there was any place in it for pain and disaster. If God is perceived as a God of success who fixes things when they need fixing and turns life into a harmonious party, there is a large part of human experience from which the creator is excluded.

It is not my intention to prick the bubble of joy that

conversion brings. New life is to be celebrated and shared. The zealous witness to life-transforming faith is commendable (though it may sometimes turn away cautious seekers after truth). But Jeremiah, like so many of God's people whose stories are told in the scriptures, testifies to the struggle and apparent failure that often accompany faithful living of the message. As he came to know the truth about God, himself and his nation, he grew more isolated from most of those who surrounded him. Truth is a divider. It is easier to choose false peace, to complacently support obsolete structures, or to hold on to an image of God that will not disturb. The messenger who disturbs this state of things can expect hostility, but will continue to speak silently by the integrity of his or her life. Testimony to the transforming power of God in human experience has a much sharper ring of truth when it encompasses the disappointments, loss of certainty, and misunderstanding which accrue from faithfulness to the message. Pilate asked the question "What is truth?" and then crucified the Truth standing before him. The messenger and the message were so fused that he hoped the death of one would silence the other. How wrong he was!

A Journal Reflection

The prophet Habakkuk was able to give thanks to God who enabled him to express faith in the future even though prosperity and success were not guaranteed. Take a few moments to recall the times when life has been disappointing, friends have disappeared, loved ones have misunderstood and God has seemed far away. Using the psalm as a pattern, write your own version, encompassing the things which are important in your life and expressing trust in the faithfulness of God.

O Lord, I have heard of your renown,
  your work, O Lord, inspires me with dread.
In the midst of the years you made yourself known,
  and in wrath you remembered mercy.
God comes from Teman,
  the Holy One from Mount Paran;
His radiance overspreads the skies,
  and his splendor fills the earth.
He goes forth to save his people;
  he comes to save his anointed.
Although the figtree does not blossom,
  the vines bear no fruit, the olive crop fails,
the orchards yield no food,
  the fold is bereft of its flock
  and there are no cattle in the stalls,
yet I will exult in the Lord,
  and rejoice in the God of my deliverance.
The Lord is my strength
  who makes my feet nimble as a mountain goat's,
  and sets me to range the heights.[1]

The verses at the beginning of this chapter are from one of Jeremiah's "confessions." These poetic cries of anguish to God erupt from the heart-searching of the prophet as he lays bare his deepest fears and pain. The longer passages of this type are found in 11:18-12:6; 15:10-11, 21; 17:14-18; 18:18-23; 20:7-18, and there are two more short poems in 5:3-5 and 8:18-23. These will be considered further in chapter 6, but they are relevant here because they reveal how inseparable Jeremiah was from the message he proclaimed.

Jeremiah speaks in 4:11-18 of the catastrophe that will overwhelm Judah, comparing the invading armies to the scorching sirocco wind that roars in from the desert.

It is a wind too strong for winnowing, for it snatches both wheat and chaff together in its burning fury. No discrimination is possible; both good and bad are caught up in its destructive power, and so it will be with God's "daughter," the people of Judah. All will be subject to the terrible judgment coming through Babylonian conquest. Having uttered this fearful message, Jeremiah experiences the intense pain of his call. He knows that he must announce destruction and judgment—he must pluck up, cast down and destroy the way things are. At the same time he loves his own people deeply, and longs to offer a different message. So he cries out "My anguish, my anguish! I writhe in pain" or, as the older King James translation has it: "My bowels, my bowels! I am pained at my very heart." Ancient psychology readily associated disturbed emotional experience with the organs affected, and the expression indicates the intensity of Jeremiah's suffering. He could not remain theoretical about the vision of coming judgment but must enter into it, sharing the terrible sense of defenselessness it brought:

> Suddenly, in an instant, his flimsy shelter was thrown down and its curtains torn to shreds. He was isolated and swallowed up in the storm which he had called upon the land in God's name. He wondered how much longer he could stand the emotional strain of it all, witnessing the standard of the enemy raised high and hearing the sound of the trumpet blasts.[2]

The external disarray was completely interwoven with an internal anguish that seemed unendurable.

In his book *The Sign of Jonas*[3] Thomas Merton sees life as a whale of a paradox, and so it is. Paradox lies at the

heart of Jeremiah and his message. In many ways an intro-
verted contemplative, he was compelled to take an un-
popular public stand and to suffer the consequences. A
man of passionate love for God's people, he proclaimed to
them Yahweh's word of doom and destruction. Raised in a
priestly family, he was called into the prophetic role, and
the work of hopeful building and planting was accomplished only after pulling down and tearing up. As a result
of his obedience to God, Jeremiah often experienced desolation and the absence of divine comfort. His ministry
plunged him into the depths of despair and yet somehow
he found the faith to go on proclaiming the hopeful future
lying beyond inevitable destruction.

Christ, the prince of peace, unequivocally told his
followers that his coming brought not peace but a sword.
The truth that divides is combative. All who embrace it,
who incarnate and proclaim it, can expect to be wounded
and to experience the paradox which is central to authentic living. In contrast to the preacher who declares:
"Come to Christ and your problems will be solved," Jeremiah would invite us to see and hear God's call and then
live our way into its painful but hope-filled consequences.

Shortly after he had founded the Society of St. John
the Evangelist, Richard Meux Benson was asked: "Well,
Father, have you found peace?" "No," he replied, "I have
found war!" The choice of monastic poverty and a life
devoted to prayer is not about withdrawal from the world
but engagement with it; it means a consent to deep and
dangerous encounter with all that is hostile to the gospel
of Christ. The monk, like the prophet, is a sign of paradox,
and every Christian, by virtue of baptism, is called to live
paradoxically. The greatest paradox of all is the cross of
Christ, instrument of torture and scandal but also symbol
of resurrection and new life. Taking up the cross in order

to follow involves entering into its scandal. It means that we take our place with Christ against the deadness of a tradition which refuses to open itself to the fresh breeze of the Spirit. And those who hold power over the crumbling structures of prejudice and fear will do all they can to deny the message and annihilate the messenger.

A Journal Dialogue

When Jeremiah felt abandoned, and resistant to the pain of his vocation, he entered into dialogue with God. He was not afraid to be truly honest with his creator or to use metaphors that were somewhat shocking. At one point he describes God as a brook that has run dry just at the time when thirst-quenching water is needed (Jer 15:18). Remembering some of those personal times of pain and loss, and recalling any present sense of anguish, begin to enter into a dialogue with God about the experience of isolation. As images of God emerge, even if they seem shocking, allow them to be expressed. When you have finished, take a few moments to reflect on the feelings generated by this exercise. Was there relief or fear? release or guilt? any new sense of who God is for you? End with a prayer, written or spoken silently, as a response to where you are at this moment.

Twentieth Century Prophets

The late Colin O'Brien Winter, exiled bishop of Namibia, was a more recent prophet in whom the message of judgment, liberation and hope was embodied. I first met him some three years before his death, when he came to preach and celebrate the eucharist in my parish in

southeast London. He shocked and disturbed our comfortable Anglican worship that Sunday morning, asking of
us a commitment and spontaneity to the Word which sets
people free. Expelled by the government of South West
Africa for his refusal to implement the dehumanizing policies of apartheid in his diocese, he established the International Namibian Peace Center in the east end of London,
and continued for several years to be bishop in exile. He
had one message. Oppression is evil—Christ came to set
all people free, and we make liberation a reality when we
take our place alongside our poor, afflicted and disenfranchised sisters and brothers.

Colin disturbed our orderly liturgy and he deeply disturbed the unjust government of Namibia. He disturbed
the Church of England too, not only by his refusal of a
"comfortable" job, but by his public challenge of its investments in South Africa. He took his uncompromising
message to the United Nations, he traveled widely raising
funds in the western world to support those struggling for
freedom in southern Africa, and he was a prolific writer.
The powers-that-be in church and government were embarrassed by his outspoken challenges which went on like
an irritating, scratching soundtrack of an old phonograph
when the needle sticks in a groove. There were those who
loved him and shared his very modest living space at the
Peace Center. The unemployed, poorly housed Cockney
men and women with whom he worked in solidarity
against unscrupulous landowners knew him as a friend.
Many whose commitment to the church as an institution
was tenuous discovered an authentic living of the gospel
and came to share the meal and simple eucharistic celebration which was characteristic of the community. Africans seeking education and freedom from oppressive

regimes made their home temporarily with him while they studied and prepared to go back to work for freedom among their own people.

Like Jeremiah, Colin Winter sometimes engaged in shocking demonstrations of his message. One day, discovering oranges bearing the designation "Outspan" in the house, he went outside and hurled them one by one across the street where they formed a mushy pile in the gutter. Nothing produced at the expense of others' freedom was knowingly allowed in the house. His vestments were colorful, beaded and African made, in contrast to the sober and expensive garments worn in most British churches, and his crozier was a hand carved, simple wooden cane. He was always a surprise, and it was impossible to escape the challenge of his message. Exhausted by unremitting travel and speaking engagements, he suffered several heart attacks and finally died in November 1981 at the age of fifty-three. He was to have been the preacher at my ordination to the priesthood in December of that year, though it was clear several months before that he would not be well enough to cross the Atlantic. The support he gave, and his solidarity with me in what he described as the "apartheid" of the Church of England in refusing to test my vocation because of gender, are engraved indelibly on my memory. In remarkable ways he enabled me to claim some of my own freedom and to live out the consequences.

Colin's ashes remain in England as he instructed, and will be returned to Namibia only when its people finally gain freedom. He was the message. He suffered profoundly the pain of exile from those he loved and, like Jeremiah, found some solace in the poetry he wrote while he wept and agonized for them. He was often alone with his grief,

sometimes feeling abandoned by the God who called him
to pastor the afflicted. The Rt. Rev. Jim Thompson, then
bishop of Stepney, said following the announcement of
Colin Winter's death:

> In a sense he was a very discomforting person
> because he had no truck with compromise, and
> so he made people face the deep, underlying
> principles. He was that sort of prophet: people
> took against him, or those who heard and be-
> lieved had to rethink what they were doing, and
> what they were believing in. It's so easy for the
> institutional Church to be on the side of power,
> and he wasn't on the side of power, so he didn't
> fit in well in the C. of E.[4]

Jeremiah experienced very little of "success" in his
lifetime. He entered into God's suffering over the broken
covenant with Judah, yet never "slides over to God's side
of the equation. The combative distance between Yahweh
and Israel is and remains a combative distance also for
Jeremiah."[5] The prophet was subjected to and submerged
by the crisis of the broken covenant, and out of the anguish of distance from God and people he spoke and lived.
He stands as a witness to us. We are called to recognize the
enemies of truth, the foe that marches with the iron feet of
violence and oppression, and to challenge its insidious
power. Even while our cry of aloneness rings in God's
ears, we hold on to faith that a new world is being built
out of the broken ruins.

The acted parables in the book of Jeremiah make the
message more scandalously real. The drama of the smashed
flask (Jer 19), with the prediction of the shattering of

God's people by the invading armies of Babylon, enraged
those who heard. Shortly afterward Jeremiah was beaten
by the priest, Pashur, and placed in the stocks at the Benjamin gate, to suffer public disgrace and ridicule (Jer 20:
1-2). We have already considered the symbol of the yoke
which he wore to reinforce his message of coming bondage under the enemy. At the very moment the Babylonian
armies were besieging Jerusalem and real estate was
worthless, Jeremiah bought a field in Anathoth from his
cousin Hanamel (Jer 32:1f). The deeds were carefully
drawn up, sealed, and placed in an earthen vessel to last
for a long time. Thus in the midst of disaster he proclaimed, by his actions, confidence in the God of compassion who would ultimately restore this land and the
covenant people.

Our pragmatic culture might well pose the question,
"But what good did it do?" After all, the exile happened as
predicted. Jeremiah suffered with the people of God, and
warning them of impending disaster only brought him
hostility and rejection. Do smashed vases and oranges actually achieve anything? The first answer to the question is
that God calls us to discipleship and faithfulness whether
the message "works" or not. The prophets speak and act
not because they choose to do so but because they cannot
do anything else. Integrity is at stake; they know the truth
must be expressed, and its consequences are not their
business. The second answer has to do with the impact of
the message long after it has been spoken. Jeremiah was
part of the building and planting as he encouraged the
exiles to accept the present while preparing for the future
envisaged by the deeded field. And he "speaks" to us in a
very different time and culture of the need to let go of
complacent idolatry as we struggle to discern the real

essence of faith. When my fear of ridicule holds me back from some action or challenge, I remember Bishop Colin Winter, and his spirit lives in me as I find the courage to do what is difficult. The whole Christian story, with its martyrs and witnesses throughout the centuries, speaks of the living, energizing power of the living Christ to change people and nations.

At a conference in California in 1985,[6] Matthew Fox defined a prophet as "one who interferes," and he went on to challenge us with the questions: "What have you interfered with in your life? What is God telling you to interfere with at this moment?" Those who have gone to jail for sitting on railroad tracks to prevent the passage of trains carrying hazardous nuclear waste through populated areas, or for harboring refugees fleeing violent oppression, or for symbolic acts of violence against weapon installations, have interfered with policies they believe to be unjust or evil. The people who place themselves between trawlers hunting whales to extinction and those graceful, gentle creatures of the deep are interfering with an economy based on indiscriminate slaughter and are making a statement about responsible stewardship of God's creation. Those who refuse to engage in sharp business practices or the exploitation of the masses through investments in an advertising industry which bases its success on greed and guilt soon find themselves pilloried for their moral scruples. It is not immediately obvious that their actions achieve anything, though the effects may be far deeper than they realize when they are enduring the public humiliation of their call. When messenger and message become one, it is impossible not to hear. A song written some twenty years after the execution of the labor leader Joe Hill tells of the enduring impact of his life and

willingness to die for freedom and equitable wages and
working conditions:

> I dreamed I saw Joe Hill last night
> Alive as you and me.
> Says I, "But Joe, you're ten years dead!"
> "I never died," says he.
> "I never died," says he.
>
> "In Salt Lake, Joe, by God," says I,
> Him standing by my bed,
> "They framed you on a murder charge."
> Says Joe, "But I ain't dead."
> Says Joe, "But I ain't dead."
>
> "The copper bosses killed you, Joe.
> They shot you, Joe," says I.
> "Takes more than guns to kill a man,"
> says Joe, "I didn't die,"
> says Joe, "I didn't die."
>
> And standing there as big as life
> and smiling with his eyes,
> Joe says, "What they forgot to kill
> Went on to organize
> Went on to organize."
>
> "Joe Hill ain't dead," he says to me,
> "Joe Hill ain't never died
> Where working men are out on strike
> Joe Hill is at their side,
> Joe Hill is at their side."

"From San Diego up to Maine
In every mine and mill
Where workers strike and organize,"
Says he, "You'll find Joe Hill."
Says he, "You'll find Joe Hill."

I dreamed I saw Joe Hill last night
Alive as you and me.
Says I, "But Joe, you're ten years dead."
"I never died," says he.
"I never died," says he.[7]

The author of the book of Hebrews offers a long list of men and women of faith who lived without knowing the full impact of their lives on those who came after. This great "cloud of witnesses" by which we are surrounded invites us by their testimony and fidelity, to let go of the heavy weight of sin and fear, and to take our place as those who also run with perseverance "looking to Jesus, the pioneer and perfecter of our faith" (Heb 12:1–2). Embodying the message of the gospel, standing firm for freedom and wholeness, we place ourselves in that prophetic tradition that risks finding God in the dark places as we learn to interfere with all that diminishes human dignity and God's glory.

Journal Exercises

1. Read Hebrews 11 slowly and thoughtfully. What qualities are revealed in the lives of these people of faith? Are there attitudes you want to emulate or fresh directions you need to take? Record your response.

2. Have you encountered "prophets" in your own time? If
    so, describe them and consider their continuing im-
    pact on your life.

3. Look back over your life and recall occasions when you
    have "interfered" with a situation, belief system, or tra-
    dition. What feelings were associated with your action?
    How did you deal with them?

4. Consider your present life situation and ask whether
    there is anything God is asking you to do or say which is
    in the prophetic tradition. If there is, journal with your-
    self about how you will go about it, where you will find
    support, and how you will deal with misunderstanding.

5

Hope

I know the plans I have for you, says the Lord,
plans for welfare and not for evil, to give you a
future and a hope (Jer 29:11).

*T*he history recorded in both Hebrew and Christian
scriptures is oriented toward the future. It looks forward
with hope to what is not yet, while remaining firmly
rooted in the present. Eschatology, the doctrine of the last
things, though it developed and changed with time, is a
constituent of the interpretation of this history from earliest times. The story of Abraham and Sarah leaving the
security of home for the risk of nomadic wanderings in
response to inner promptings is a story of hope resting on
God's promises. Hope was not mere optimism but the gift
of God sealed by covenant (cf. Gen 12:1-3; 15:7-21). It
was that sense of covenant ratified on Mount Sinai which
provided the basis of the nation's hope.

Journal Reflection

Take a few moments to reflect on the verse at the
beginning of this chapter. Read it several times and hear
it as spoken, by God, to you. Be aware of your feelings as
you are assured of a future and a hope. Now draw a line
graph indicating your life experience. Mark the times

when you were most hopeful. Journal with your thoughts and thanksgivings about those times.

The Hope of Israel

In Jeremiah 14:8 the prophet addresses God as "the hope of Israel." This occurs in a passage where lament in times of drought and national defeat is the focus. A situation of national disaster and political oppression calls out from him an affirmation of God's future in which the people will share. He enables them to envision something better than their present experience contains, and provides the energy needed to go on. In using this designation for God, Jeremiah stands in the mainstream of Hebrew thought, for God and hope were so closely associated as to be almost synonymous. We have already seen how hope was embedded in the call of Jeremiah when he learned that his task was not only to pluck up, break down, destroy and overthrow, but also to build and to plant. Hope was necessary as preparation for the future took place.

Hope and judgment are the essence of the covenant relationship. The promise that God cares and will intervene on behalf of the community carries responsibility. A people so favored must be threatened by judgment if they fail to keep the covenant and descend into egotism and a narrow nationalism. Jeremiah needed to confront the complacent self-satisfaction which blinded God's people to the impending peril from the north, the enemy which would be the instrument of divine judgment. He called on them to wake up to reality, to repent, and to recognize that judgment is the inevitable consequence of infidelity. However to speak only of judgment would lead to despair, so even in the darkest times the light of hope filters through.

> This note of judgment is nothing different from
> the vision of hope. It is simply the other side of
> the single reality. To cherish hope is not to es-
> cape into dream and fantasy. It is . . . to embrace
> that which is difficult but possible to attain—
> possible because there is a righteous God at work
> in the world . . . who is the "hope of Israel."[1]

The verse at the beginning of this chapter comes from
a letter which Jeremiah wrote to encourage the exiles in
Babylon. The terrible things he had predicted came to
pass, and many were now relocated in an alien land. Conditions under Babylonian rule were not as harsh as those
under the Assyrians, and Jeremiah encourages the people
to settle down, build houses, plant vineyards and go on
with normal family life. He indicates that the period of
exile will be long enough to establish new forms of community, and in caring about the welfare of their captors
God's people will find their own welfare. Israel will rediscover its identity by committing itself to the future while
living with the present reality and accepting what has
gone before.

Chapter 29 of Jeremiah is a lengthy prose section
containing letters sent between Jerusalem and Babylon. A
letter from Jeremiah to the exiles is found in verses 1–15,
21–23, and 25–28, where he reports the contents of one
from Shemaiah, in Babylon, to Zephaniah. Another letter
from Jeremiah to the exiles appears at the end of the chapter (vv. 31f). At this time Israel was in danger of losing its
identity as a nation. Far from home the observances and
rhythms of life which bound them together had come to
an end. The temple, center of national identity, was destroyed, and there appeared to be no future for them as
the covenant community. Into this scene the false proph-

ets were ready to inject optimism based on their predictions of an early end to Babylonian rule. Once again Jeremiah found himself in opposition to their facile and empty words. Yahweh had a lesson for the people to learn through suffering, and they would not learn it through escapism. Exile represented the judgment of God on a people who had forsaken the covenant, but it was also a means through which restoration and renewal might take place following an honest recognition of sin, repentance, and return to God. It also meant a broadening of their vision of God's rule to include these whom they designated enemies.

The hope which Jeremiah offered to the exiles was not tied into an early return to the land of their origins. It was firmly based on the conviction that God was with them in the place of exile, enabling them to live and rebuild community. They were being invited to let go of an exclusive view of God, of dependence on external supports for their faith, and to enter into a fresh search for truth. Hope lay in the renewal of religion which God would accomplish in them through their willing obedience:

> Behold, the days are coming, says the Lord, when I will make a new covenant with the house of Judah, not like the covenant which I made with their fathers when I took them by the hand to bring them out of the land of Egypt, my covenant which they broke, though I was their husband, says the Lord. But this is the covenant which I will make with the house of Israel after these days, says the Lord: I will put my law within them, and I will write it upon their hearts; and I will be their God, and they shall be my people (Jer 31: 31–33).

Healing and reconciliation became the foundation of hope for those willing to learn the lessons of the present moment.

Journal Questions

1. Are there situations about which you are tempted to feel hopeless at this time? If so, identify them, and ask yourself how you might turn fearful anticipation into hope as you bring these things into the orbit of faith. What do you need from God? Be specific about your prayer as you journal your response.

2. As you begin each day, make a determination to look for signs of hope in the world. Notice items in the media, meetings with people, moments of surprise when hope replaces fear. Record your observations.

Envisioning the Future

Walter Brueggeman calls his book on the exilic prophets Jeremiah, Ezekiel, and Second Isaiah *Hopeful Imagination*. He sees their task as that of helping God's people to enter into exile, to be in exile, and to depart out of exile. This task is accomplished through powerful prophetic imagination, for they not only discerned the new actions of God to which others were blind, they brought about those actions through their imagination and by the spoken and written word. Jeremiah's poetic insight generated hope following the climactic events of 587 B.C.

Jeremiah's vitality comes precisely from his passionate conviction about the power of God to work a newness in the zero hours of loss and exile. Jeremiah does not believe that the world is hopelessly closed so that living is only moving the pieces around. Jeremiah believes that God is able to do an utterly new thing which violates our reason, our control and our despair. Jeremiah bears witness to the work of God, the capacity to bring newness ex nihilo. For that reason loss and emptiness are not the last word.[2]

When Rev. Dr. Martin Luther King, Jr. made his now famous "I Have a Dream" speech, he was not only challenging the racism that many considered an unchanging fact of life, he was envisioning new possibilities. Into a climate of fear-ridden acquiescence to the way things were he injected hope. It was hope, not fear, he said that was needed if blacks in the U.S.A. were to claim their inalienable right to equality and freedom. People were tired of being trampled by the "iron feet of oppression" and they needed a prophetic voice that would encourage them to image a hopeful future. Like Jeremiah he found himself the target of those who spoke in the name of God and nation, supporting the status quo. And he paid with his life for his message.

The authentic prophet is always concerned with enabling people to come to fresh visions of reality, and to redefine their experience. Moses, reluctant as Jeremiah to respond to God's call, was not only to intervene between the oppressed Israelites and Pharaoh. His continuing task was to inject enough hope into God's people to make the exodus a possibility and to keep them moving. Hopelessness was the great enemy of progress. The Red Sea, hunger and thirst in the desert, and enemy threat appeared as specters of fear during those forty years of wandering.

There were always those ready to give up, and always God provided a new way of seeing the future. On the border of the promised land the people received reports of how Canaan looked to the spies who entered it. One group returned with tales of the strength of its inhabitants, and prediction of defeat for Israel who were "like grasshoppers" in comparison. A minority opinion, offered by Joshua and Caleb, painted a different picture. The land was "an exceedingly good land," and if God was delighted with Israel, there was no question about their success in taking it. Hope lay not in human strength alone but in the presence of the God who had delivered them from Egypt and kept them through their desert wanderings. The God of hope, their defender, was always ahead of them, and knowing that reduced human strength to appropriate proportions.

One of our great needs today, in a world gripped by fear, is to make possible a different vision of reality. What would happen if, instead of stockpiling nuclear arsenals, the super-powers looked beyond themselves to a new world—a global village at peace? As long as we are content to project evil onto the enemy and complacently claim God and right as our own, that vision is not possible. Where would we be if our churches ceased protecting themselves against different expressions of faith by claiming that they alone had the truth, and, instead, opened themselves to the richness of other traditions? What would happen in our personal lives if, instead of fearfully protecting our fragile egocentric existence, we confronted the enemy within and envisioned ourselves as the whole persons God destined us to become? Hope is the vehicle of transformation that tells us the future is possible.

T.S. Eliot was right when he suggested that we cannot

bear too much reality, but that does not mean we have to opt for a fantasy world. We can begin to let go of cynicism and hopelessness bit by bit as we allow the God of hope to address us. Many letters and much encouragement were offered before the exiles arrived at a place where they were willing to relinquish old ways of thinking and relating in order to receive a new life. There were other voices besides that of Jeremiah to support this process, but they had to tune out the ever present prognostications of those who refused the vision. At some point during this period a new sense of community came into being and the synagogue was born. The word literally translated means "gathering together," and it is that coming to meet in common worship that has sustained Jewish people through many centuries of antisemitism since. This was part of the new vision, and it meant that when return to Israel took place, a tradition and a way of life were not lost.

Léon Joseph Cardinal Suenens was once asked by the editor of *The Critic* why, in spite of the confusion of our time, he is a man of hope. His reply is printed in the Preface of his book *New Pentecost:*

> Because I believe that God is born anew each morning, because I believe that he is creating the world at this very moment. He did not create it at a distant and long-forgotten moment of time. It is happening now; we must therefore be ready to expect the unexpected from God. The ways of Providence are by nature surprising. We are not prisoners of determinism nor of the sombre prognostications of sociologists. God is here, near us, unforeseeable and loving. I am a man of hope, not for any human reasons nor from any

natural optimism, but because I believe the Holy
Spirit is at work in the Church and in the world,
even where his name remains unheard. I am an
optimist because I believe the Holy Spirit is the
Spirit of creation. To those who welcome him he
gives each day fresh liberty and renewed joy and
trust. . . . I believe in the surprises of the Holy
Spirit. . . . To hope is a duty, not a luxury. To hope
is not to dream, but to turn dreams into reality.
Happy are those who dream dreams and are
ready to pay the price to make them come true.
(Pentecost 1974)[3]

Our Christian hope is founded not on natural optimism but on the faithfulness of a God who called the
world into being and gave us life. This God of hope jour-
neys with us through all the vicissitudes of our pilgrimage
and constantly renews our vision of reality. Hope is God's
gift to us and the gift we have to offer in a world where
despair is always threatening to paralyze people into in-
action. Like Jeremiah, and all those who have found the
courage to engage in combat with fear or disillusionment,
we can dream dreams believing that the God of hope will
enable us to pay what it costs to turn those dreams into
reality.

Mrs. Corazon Aquino, speaking in New York at Mount
St. Vincent's College shortly after her election as presi-
dent of the Philippines, offered her definition of faith. She
might well have been speaking for Jeremiah: "Faith is not
simply a patience which passively suffers until the storm is
past. Rather, it is a spirit which bears all things—with
resignation, yes, but above all with blazing, serene hope."
Hope accepts the reality of the present, even when that
reality is painful, but it does not wring its hands. Instead it

keeps in view new possibilities, new ways of being that will be available only when the past is relinquished. The timeless God is the absolute source of such daring hope.

More Journal Questions

1. What are your dreams for the future? How can you become a part of the fulfillment of those dreams? What price will you have to pay to realize them? Is it worth it?

2. Reflect on the people you have known personally or have heard about who embodied hope. Write a description of one such person and ask yourself if there are some attitudes and qualities which you want to embrace as your own.

3. Read Romans 15:13. Reflect on ways in which God *has* filled you with hope and on how you might more fully enter into that hope. Pray for those who need the gift of faith and hope at this time.

6

Exile

> King Nebuchadrezzar . . . entered Jerusalem. And
> he burned the house of the Lord, and the king's
> house and all the houses of Jerusalem; every great
> house he burned down. And all the army of the
> Chaldeans, who were with the captain of the
> guard, broke down all the walls round about
> Jerusalem. And Nebuzaradan the captain of the
> guard carried away captive some of the poorest
> of the people who were left in the city and the
> deserters who had deserted to the king of Baby-
> lon, together with the rest of the artisans. But
> Nebuzaradan the captain of the guard left some
> of the poorest of the land to be vinedressers and
> plowmen (Jer 52:12-16).

*T*he experience of exile is excruciatingly painful. To be
cut off from one's roots, bereft of home and heritage,
adrift in an unknown ocean of darkness, is a dreadfully
lonely experience. All the familiar patterns which sustain
life are gone. So are the comfortable people, the regular
rituals both personal and communal, and all that gives
shape to existence and provides rhythm for being. Exile
means disorientation and a loss of the equilibrium for
which we all long. It compels us to ask the most fundamental questions about who we are—questions which

much of the time we avoid by clinging to the familiar. To be an exile is to be in question and to have no certainty that there will ever again be a place we can call home.

Such was the experience of God's people when the Babylonians finally succeeded in their attempts to capture Jerusalem. The year 587 B.C. marks a pivotal moment in history; it represents the ending of an era and ultimately became the beginning point for a new definition of the covenant community. But in between lay the difficult struggle for survival—not physical survival, since the Babylonians were not unduly harsh in their treatment of captive people, but the survival of national identity. At the beginning of Zedekiah's reign in 597 B.C., a small but significant number of people were deported to Babylon, most of them key figures in Judah's administration. A number of plots and rebellions followed, some of them probably supported by those already in exile, and then King Zedekiah himself rebelled. Babylon acted swiftly. By January 588 B.C. Jerusalem was under siege, but instead of attacking the city immediately, the Babylonians set about destroying other fortified cities throughout Judah. Hope of relief offered by the Egyptian army who arrived in the summer of that year was short-lived, though Jeremiah indicates that many expected victory (cf. Jer 37:3–10).

The lifting of the siege of Jerusalem was brief, and the walls of the city were breached just as food supplies ran out. Zedekiah and his family fled by night but were quickly captured, his sons killed before his eyes, and the king himself blinded before being taken in chains to Babylon. One month later Nebuzaradan took the city. The predictions of Jeremiah came to pass. Those who relied on the temple of the Lord saw it razed to the ground, desecrated with fire, and all the great houses of Jerusalem destroyed. Some of the poor who remained, artisans, and those who had already seen the writing on the wall and deserted to the king of Babylon were taken into captivity. A disenchanted, disparate and frightened group of former Judeans were now thrown together on alien soil. It seemed unlikely that anything new could come from such a spiritually, psychologically and physically defeated people, yet exile proved to be the seedbed of new life.

We have already seen how Jeremiah acted pastorally to enable the people of Judah to rediscover hope and to survive the exile (Jer 29:11). Earlier in the letter to the exiles he advised: "Build houses and live in them; plant gardens and eat their produce. Take wives and have sons and daughters; take wives for your sons and give your daughters in marriage that they may bear sons and daughters; multiply there and do not decrease" (Jer 29:5-6). Jeremiah not only indicated that the exile would consume a lengthy period of time, but he also helped the people to enter into that experience. Not in denial of the present but in an embracing of its painful ambiguity lay the hope of the nation. As they became accustomed to life in an alien land, seeking the welfare of those who were initially seen as the enemy, they were to discover new patterns of community.

Perhaps Jeremiah was able to speak with confidence and hope of the experience of exile because, in the acceptance of his vocation, he had already learned its lesson for himself. His words, running counter to the predominant religious and cultural message of his day, alienated him from those with whom he would normally have identified. His was a lonely task, and he suffered the loss of friends, family and temple, becoming "homeless" even while he dwelt in Judah. Like those in Babylon, he knew what it was to yearn for escape at any cost, craving the familiar routines, tempted to refuse the lessons of loss.

But he remained true to his call, not without complaint, yet breaking through the engulfing waves of fear again and again. His experience qualified him to support the exiles through fear to new faith.

For most of us a major uprooting such as that endured by Israel is unlikely to be part of experience, though perhaps our forebears went through a similar experience in their quest for freedom. Nevertheless, that feeling of alienation, of not belonging, is common to all. Prior to my fifth birthday, I entered school in a small village in England where children of several grades were taught in the same class. I felt frightened and very alone in that class, not knowing where to sit, unable to read the word card others had mastered, not yet a part of the community. When I could not find a chair on my second day, the teacher marched me around by the scruff of the neck, to point out the pile of stacked chairs behind the piano! There was a kind of folk law I had to master, and it included knowing where to find one's chair at the beginning of the day. It took time before I could settle down there. I had no desire to "build houses and dwell in them," and I wanted only to escape the hostile place. I indicated my rejection of the place dramatically by hurling across the floor the doll the teacher gave me to hold because I cried so much!

That childhood experience represents the first memory of feelings of exile, but by no means the last. Another occurred when I entered college at the age of twenty-two and joined a class of high school graduates. I had worked for a number of years, supported myself, and now felt very excited about the opportunities offered by education. Most of those in my class were tired of school, so their goals were primarily to have a good time, find plenty of dates, and end up with a diploma which they might use briefly before marriage and motherhood. The four year age difference between us appeared much greater as I listened to their conversations and felt that I inhabited a different world.

Perhaps the most acute sense of exile developed when I recognized for the first time that, as a woman, I was not valued as an equal in the church. For seven years I taught in a British seminary, and during that time a sense of call to ordained ministry grew. I observed the discriminatory practices which women students endured, and their conditioning to accept these as "normal." It went far beyond the college community and certainly included employment opportunities. I had been conditioned for years myself, assuming there were roles which were just not appropriate for women, and accepting the way things were. The inner conviction that I should be a priest was aided by those who were affirming my call and asking for a sacramental ministry I could not offer. The awareness of oppression caused a deepening sense of alienation from those who did not recognize or support it. Many of them were women with strongly held convictions that the church was right in denying ordination to those of their gender. I felt like an exile in my own church and community. Finding the courage to speak out, and to expose injustice, was a continuing struggle, yet one about which I felt I had no option. I think I felt closest to Jeremiah in his personal prophetic stance at this time, and I certainly needed his cries of rage and lament as models for my prayer.

Journal Reflection

Return to the graph on which you noted moments of hope on your personal journey. This time, indicate times when you felt "cut off" from your roots. Journal your memories of these experiences and express your feelings. Where was God during those times? Take as much time as you need for this exercise.

The next suggestion may be appropriate for a later occasion, and it is important not to rush through it, so be aware of how and when you need to approach it. Psalm 137 comes from the time of the exile and expresses the anguish of God's people. Read it meditatively as you did with the psalm of Habakkuk. Ask God to show you if there is some loss you need to bring into your prayer in order to find healing. Using Psalm 137 as a model, write your own psalm expressing feelings of loss and bereavement. Don't be afraid to express the vindictive, resentful thoughts. God is able to receive and deal with these parts of ourselves, and we can trust in divine mercy and grace for ourselves and those we hate. Harboring anger is much more destructive than allowing it to be shared by God; by expressing rage or vindictiveness, we are enabled to let go and find hope.

New Roots

Prophets are subversive. They disturb current perceptions of the way things are and suggest, often through dramatic metaphor and symbol, that radical rethinking is necessary. Yokes, broken pots, loincloths buried in the earth, all "speak" powerfully Jeremiah's word from the Lord. A beam in the eye of one attempting to remove a speck of sawdust from the eye of another; the ludicrous spectacle of a camel being pushed through the eye of a needle; quarreling children at play in the market place—all announce with biting clarity the message of Jesus. But the important, continuing task of the prophet is to help those who hear articulate for themselves the truth for their age. Out of the past new hopes are born, but only when there is a letting go of what is now obsolete so that what is new may be embraced. And it is all important for the new community to speak into reality what they understand, for no parroting of the words of prophet or guru will activate that reality.

The experience of exile provides an opportunity to discover God's presence in the chaotic, disoriented parts of life. As we have already observed, Christian belief is sometimes presented as a panacea to life's ills, and God is identified as the provider of peace and happiness. Jeremiah will not let us escape the sobering fact that much of the time being human means dealing with chaos, confusion, and limitation, and authentic faith learns to find God in the disturbed places. Though the Hebrews longed for peace as much as any of us, they were much more ready to find God in darkness and distress than we tend to be. The Psalms bear eloquent witness to the cries of anguish wrung from individual and nation struggling with the fear generated by dislocation and rootlessness. Healing and insight grew as fears were expressed and the present, painful moment opened to the possibility of God's action. God was invited to participate in the anguish and expected to respond to the needs of the sufferer(s).

Journaling is one way we can give speech to the exile experience and, in time, discover some form in it. My own journal, covering a particularly lonely, stressful period of time, ultimately became a book, and the writing of it was amazingly therapeutic.[1] In 1981 I left my native England and asked the Episcopal Church in the United States to test my vocation to the priesthood. My self-imposed exile began with much sadness at the loss of home but was also filled with hopeful anticipation as the fulfillment of my call drew near. In the first months I was busy planning the ordination, adjusting to full-time parish ministry, meeting new friends and enjoying all the benefits of life in the United States. When my first appointment came to an end I moved to New York City in order to complete studies for a further graduate degree and to look for a new position. It was then, more than a year after I had left England, that I began to deal with the painful sense of loss, of not really belonging in that teeming, vibrant, exciting and tough city. Uncertain whether I would be able to pay the rent each month, without a permanent parish appointment, and now distant from the friends I had made in New Jersey, I was thoroughly lonely and dislocated. Who was I? Had the move to America been a mistake? Would people here want what I had to offer, or would I join the ranks of the unemployed clergy? Where was God?

I journaled my fear and disappointment. I remembered the clarity with which I had chosen to come, and occasionally I remembered God's grace in past times of loss. The little acts of trust I tried to make then required much more effort than the big decision to cross the Atlantic. These were made in the swirling mists of uncertainty, with no clear vision of the future and no assurance that things would get better. Then a dream was given to support me and renew a sense of hope. I dreamed that I was producing a play but the actors had not learned their lines. I would gather one group and find that they had left their scripts behind. Then another group appeared but their parts came much later in the play. At that moment a small goat walked on stage, and someone pointed to it and said, "You know, you should give her a much bigger part; she's very talented." I realized there was a child inside the goatskin, but dismissed the remark because I was too preoccupied with getting the play started. The same chaos continued, but I was again told to pay attention to the "goat." Then I woke up.

It is no wonder that dreams have been described as "God's forgotten language."[2] With clarity and playfulness God "spoke" to me through this dream. It accurately reflected the chaotic feelings of disorder I was experiencing and the sense that I could not get my act together! Remembering that we are participants as well as observers in our dreams, I thought about the various characters. It was true that in some sense I had not yet learned my lines—not really gotten to be at home in this country. That takes time, and my impatience was adding greatly to the stressful sense of exile. It was not yet time for the next scene, but necessary to wait out the muddle. And, of course, that was "getting my goat." At the same time, I was the little "kid," hiding in the skin playing a very small role, yet telling myself that I had talent and needed to recognize that fact. I had to hear that message twice, because I was not ready to pay attention to it the first time.

Through that dream I was learning to be in exile. That was what Jeremiah helped God's people to do, encouraging them to settle down and *be* there. He could certainly offer them encouragement that the exile would not last forever, but he was unwilling to indulge in escapism. The present was the moment of opportunity to experience God's reality. It had the potential of epiphany. Moses, "exiled" for forty years in the desert after slaying an Egyptian, felt the consuming fire of God's numinous presence and became the agent of liberation for the Hebrews. Jacob, fleeing from home and his brother's murderous wrath, heard God through a dream which assured him of the divine presence in an alien land. Esther, a Hebrew woman exiled in the harem of the Persian king, confronted her fear, stepped outside cultural gender expectations, and saved her people from extinction. And the people of Judah learned in Babylon what they would never have learned in the security of Jerusalem. God had not abandoned them, but was with them for newness.

Journal Questions

1. How do you nurture yourself when you feel alone and disoriented? Journal with ideas of good ways to live in the chaotic times without denying the difficulty of them.

2. Do you have any dreams which reflect the experience of exile? If you do not already do so, begin to record your dreams and to consider them as one of the ways in which God speaks to you. The following structure will help you in the process of understanding the messages of your dreams:

    (a) Record the dream as soon as you can on waking. Don't worry about spelling, punctuation, appearance.
    (b) Note down any emotions you felt when the dream was in progress.
    (c) List the images, metaphors, symbols that occur in it, and when you have finished the list write beside each one whatever comes to mind as you think of it. Do this quickly.
    (d) Look for puns! These can be very funny and very instructive.
    (e) Ask yourself what "day residue" might have provoked the dream. For instance an unresolved relationship which caused anxiety

might well be presented in the dream through some images you would not normally connect with the person concerned. The images are important, because they may reveal some aspects of the person which unconsciously cause problems.

(f) Look over what you have written and pray for the insight to understand more fully what the dream may be saying, and then decide how you will respond to what you now see.

Some people feel afraid of working on dreams because they are not "experts" in dream interpretation. Remember, this is *your* dream, and you are the best interpreter of the material, because you know what a particular image means to you. For example, I may experience seeing the ocean in a dream as exhilarating, while you bring to the image an experience of being overwhelmed by stormy waves. It would not be helpful for me to tell you that the ocean represents freedom, when you feel more like a drowning person. The dream has offered this image as an invitation to deal with a fearful experience and to test the reality of the fear associated with it. Healing takes place as we work prayerfully with the often hidden emotions that emerge in our dreams.

Letting Go and Going On

Exile also compels us to distinguish between what needs to remain and what must be relinquished in order for growth to happen. God's people brought with them the memory of their history. They had their rituals and their family systems. They had their political and religious leaders, their feasts and their fasts. But the temple was gone, the king was dead, and there was no cohesive community or center of worship. What was salvageable from that history? How might the essence of Hebrew faith be preserved in a foreign land? What kind of outward expression could be the means of bonding and giving voice to a new understanding of who they were? The gathering together of God's people became supremely important. The reciting and reinterpreting of past history, the learning to live without the tangible supports for faith, and an acceptance of the present led to a more inward kind of faith. People began to live their way into Jeremiah's prediction:

> Behold, the days are coming, says the Lord, when I will make a new covenant with the house of Israel and the house of Judah. . . . I will put my law within them, and I will write it upon their hearts; and I will be their God, and they shall be my people. And no longer shall each man teach his neighbor and each his brother, saying "Know the Lord," for they shall all know me, from the least of them to the greatest, says the Lord; for I will forgive their iniquity, and I will remember their sin no more (Jer 31:31, 33-34).

The sacred rolls of the Torah destroyed when the temple was razed were a monumental loss to the covenant community. But the law of God, written indelibly in their hearts, found new expression in their life together. Through exile they learned to trust in the unseen presence of the God of their forebears.

There came a time when I was ready to change my "resident alien" status and apply for American citizenship. The place of exile became "home" and, like Ruth choosing to leave her native Moab and follow her mother-in-law to Bethlehem, I could say, "Your people shall be my people." This is a country of exiles. We have come from every part of the world, bringing our traditions, and our hopes. Our history is one of struggle into freedom. My citizenship represents a willingness to build and plant—to settle down. In less dramatic ways I also found the ability to live in past exilic experience. I couldn't cope with a whole new class of children, but I could establish a few friendships which would carry me through the time of adjustment. As a "mature" college student I learned to accept my different perspectives and to value them, at the same time remaining open to learn from those who were younger. I also found other older undergraduates with whom to meet for support. When my sense of vocation remained unrecognized, joining the Movement for the Ordination of Women provided a place where like-minded people could come together, and in our meeting and working for a common cause strength was given. Our shared sense of exile led to some creative ways of worship, and some biblical images took on new power as we claimed our place in the tradition.

We come to know who we are as we touch the raw, hurting places of our lives and allow ourselves to be placed in question by the disorienting experience of marginalization. By the time the exiles were offered the freedom to return to their homeland, a strong sense of community was established. They were to need that in the face of much opposition and threat of violence as the work of rebuilding Jerusalem began. Not all chose to return. Some discovered that the place of exile had become a place where they derived energy and found the support they craved. And God was with them also.

Journaling with Today's Exiles

Jeremiah did more than talk about the problem of exile. He placed himself alongside those who suffered and gave them the support he could. Can you identify a person or group known to you for whom exile is a reality at this time? In what ways might you offer support and encouragement to them? Journal your response.

7

The Lord of Hosts

> I am called by thy name, O Lord, God of hosts. I
> did not sit in the company of merrymakers, nor
> did I rejoice; I sat alone, because thy hand was
> upon me, for thou hast filled me with indigna-
> tion. Why is my pain unceasing, my wound incur-
> able, refusing to be healed? Wilt thou be to me
> like a deceitful brook, like waters that fail? (Jer
> 15:16–18).

*T*he private prayers of Jeremiah are shocking in their
intensity and abrasiveness. For those of us conditioned
to domesticate our language so that feelings of hostility,
anger and resentment against the God who sometimes
seems to deceive us are not expressed, the candor of this
man of God may help us to a dramatic breakthrough. Jeremiah is disturbingly honest about his experience of God
and is able to use metaphors diametrically opposed to
each other when he speaks of Yahweh. On the one hand
God is described as a fountain of living water, one who re-
freshes and gives life (Jer 2:13). In the passage which begins this chapter, the prophet addresses God as a deceitful
brook, running dry when he most needs thirst-quenching
waters. Prayer grows out of experience. The tradition of
Israel, its creeds and formularies alone did not bring him

to this daring dialogue. Only the living vigorously of his vocation and the speaking candidly of its struggles gave authentic voice to his prayer.

A brief survey of those passages known as "The Confessions of Jeremiah" will help us enter into his internal anguish, and we may find echoes of our own unspoken disappointments resonating in the darkness. It is not certain when these utterances were spoken, but it is most unlikely that they were part of his public ministry. In them we feel the tension between Jeremiah the prophet, holding onto the call which he reluctantly embraced, and Jeremiah the man, shy, sensitive, and fearful of the cost of faithfulness. In responding to the divine call he might have expected Yahweh to be on his side, always vindicating him in time of trouble. In reality he was often in combat with God, pushed to the extreme of human suffering and deeply alienated from friends and Maker.

In the first of these passages (Jer 11:18–23) Jeremiah describes himself as a gentle lamb led to the slaughter, innocently subject to the betrayal and rejection of his own people. It is to the Lord of hosts that he appeals, seeking vengeance on his enemies and the vindication of his cause. This prayer turns into a dialogue, for God replies, promising to destroy those who oppress the prophet. Like Hosea whose work he seems to know, Jeremiah appeals not to a God limited to the covenant people, but to the One who is Lord of hosts. The narrow nationalism he upbraids in many of his addresses is not appropriate. Yahweh is Lord of all, who uses other nations in the fulfillment of the divine purpose, and who can act on behalf of the prophet now alienated from his own. Here Jeremiah connects us to the experience of betrayal that occurs when trust is broken, and roots are torn up as we find ourselves at odds with home and culture because of our commitment to God's way as we understand it. The rejection may be less life-threatening than that faced by Jeremiah, but the anguish remains, and the need to cry out for vindication is one step on the way to healing.

I learned to do this, hesitantly, several years ago when I was badly let down by a person in whom I had placed a great deal of trust, and with whom I had shared much of myself. At first the pain was so acute that I was unable to see any of the other good relationships that remained or to recognize God's presence in the suffering. It was not until I owned the anger, resentment and vindictiveness and allowed it into my prayer that things began to change. I was not immediately ready to forgive and to let go of my hostility, but I was back in touch with God, and my sense of who God is for me began to change. I found it really was acceptable to have the feelings that I had learned from childhood were "bad." God did not go away, but stayed with me in the raging and disappointment, and, in time, enabled me to relinquish the desire for revenge. Healing came as I waited out the chaotic, vengeful part of the experience praying for the grace to forgive, and learning to be more patient with myself, the other person and God.

Journal Question

Can you identify an experience of betrayal such as that which Jeremiah knew when his friends turned into his enemies? How did you deal with it? Is there still a need to express your feelings and pray your anger? Journal with your response, and, if it seems appropriate, write your own "confession."

Why Do the Righteous Suffer?

The second confession poses the question, "Why do bad things happen to good people?" In Jeremiah 12:1-6 the prophet not only asks why the wicked prosper, but he accuses God of planting them so that they take root and prosper. He calls upon God to pull them out, so that they will be like sheep destined for slaughter. This time there is no comforting word in reply. Instead God implies that the going will get even tougher for Jeremiah, and two power-ful metaphors are used. "If you have wearied of the foot race, how will you be able to keep up with the more de-manding charge of horses?" asks God. "If the opposition of Anathoth is too much for you, what will you do when Babylon strikes?" Jeremiah is to prepare himself for even greater conflict and not to expect an easy time. Contrary to much popular teaching that prayer makes us feel better and changes the opposition, in reality we may find our-selves more deeply embattled, needing to change from a cry for deliverance to a plea for courage to go on.

Jeremiah's perception of himself as a man of strife and contention causes him to pronounce woe on the day of his birth (Jer 15:10-12). There is more than a hint of paranoia in his confession at this point, but it would be a mistake to suggest that such psychological disturbance is not fit ma-terial for prayer. We know so much more about the human psyche than Jeremiah did, and sometimes our understand-ing can hinder rather than assist our prayers. If we become obsessed with giving names to all our neurotic responses to life, explaining them, "curing" them, but failing to allow them into the light of God's presence, we exclude a large part of ourselves from prayer. It is in the truthful expression of how we see things, even when our vision is distorted, that God hears us and does not go away.

Another dialogue between Yahweh and Jeremiah occurs in Jeremiah 15:15-21. It begins with Jeremiah's cry that he has faithfully discharged his duty despite the loneliness and opposition that involved, and he asks God to take vengeance on his enemies. Implied in this request is the conviction that the enemies are also Yahweh's enemies so that their destruction will demonstrate the sovereignty of God. Like Ezekiel (Ez 2:8-3:3), Jeremiah ate God's words and found them to be a delight and joy once they were consumed, yet his speaking of the truth caused him to be isolated—to sit alone because God's hand was heavy upon him. His pain became unbearable, his wound incurable, and he cries out *Why?* How could God do this to him? How could Yahweh "dry up" so that there was no longer any refreshment for the prophet?

Yahweh's reply is somewhat startling. Instead of receiving comfort, Jeremiah is called upon to repent, to return to God the way he had often called upon the people of Judah to return. Yahweh seems to be asking Jeremiah to turn from such talk and then God will turn back to him. The promise that Jeremiah will become "a fortified wall of bronze" against which people will fight but not prevail is closely allied to the reassurance given following his initial call to be a prophet. God does promise ultimately to deliver Jeremiah from the hand of the wicked, but it seems that first he will need to stand strong to withstand the battering of the enemy siege. Often what is needed in moments of abandonment is not a facile promise of immediate relief, but a repetition of earlier assurances. The initial call can lose its sharpness when the day by day battles cause us to feel weak and unsuccessful. The pouring out of our pain before the God who calls is met by an invitation to return and so to hear again the promise of strength for the time of struggle.

Another lament over his pain occurs in Jeremiah 17: 14–18, where the prophet asks God to heal him, confident that he will then truly be healed. There is both confidence in the power of Yahweh's healing touch, and a vindictive desire for the death of his persecutors in this prayer. We may choose to judge harshly those who express their vindictiveness in prayer. Many Christians have great problems with the imprecatory psalms and would eliminate them from the psalter as unworthy of use. Yet this is to deny the reality of the hostile hatred we bear toward those who wrong us, and to pretend that forgiveness is not costly. Psychologically and spiritually we *need* to let go of our vindictiveness before we can know healing and offer it to others. But to pretend that it does not exist is to opt for fantasy. In the expression of our desire for revenge, our murderous feelings, lies the power to change. We let go of attitudes which hurt us far more than they hurt our "enemies" only when we acknowledge their power over us and allow God to refocus our vision on our call and the divine compassion. Hatred, too, needs to be brought into our prayer, as I learned in the incident related earlier. There is no part of human experience that God will not redeem.

Journal Reflection

Go back to the stepping stones exercise at the beginning of this book. Look again at those moments when you experienced the presence of God in your personal journey. Were they all positive experiences? What images of God emerge as you look at them again? Reflect again on your life journey and see whether there were other times when you felt that God was silent, inactive, or distant but which proved to be growth points for you. Journal with your reflections.

Praying the Questions

One of the bitterest of the prophet's confessions occurs in Jeremiah 18:18-23. A grossly unjust plot against his life gives rise to a stream of cursing formulas against the aggressors. After calling on God to hear, the prophet prays that the children of his enemies may suffer famine, their wives be childless, the men meet death by pestilence and their youth be slain in battle. He asks God not to forgive their iniquity but to overthrow them. To this prayer God makes no reply. At this point Jeremiah had to live with a non-response, caught in the agony of fear as his life was threatened. Sometimes we do find ourselves in a "stuck" place, afraid for our lives. It may not be the threat of physical death, but the death of something dear to us, a relationship, a job, a dream which some catastrophe now makes impossible. At such time it may be that we have only rage to offer God, and it will seem that there is only silence in response. But the prayer has to be prayed. The alternative is a far more serious death—the death of relationship with God. As long as we are asking "My God, my God, why have you forsaken me?" (Ps 22:1), we are acknowledging that God exists, and as long as we are pouring out hatred on our enemies, we are making a tacit statement that God can act.

There is a nightmarish quality about the lamentation of Jeremiah 20:7-13, where the prophet addresses God whom he experiences as a deceiver, as one stronger than himself. Everyone seems to be laughing at the prophet, treating him as an object of reproach and derision day after day. He has a dilemma. If he stays quiet, he is burned up from inside, yet his speaking creates whispering, terror is all around, and his friends are waiting for his fall. In this recitation of dread Jeremiah finds release and hope. By the end he is reassured that God is with him as a warrior, his persecutors will be overcome, and he can sing because deliverance will come.

Sometimes the desire for equilibrium can mean a refusal to live in the chaotic oppressiveness of life which is an inevitable part of being human. In allowing the fear to be fear, even when we are over-reacting to some unnamed dread, lies hope for deliverance. The child who wakens from a bad dream cannot immediately distinguish between reality and the fearful images of the unconscious. He or she cries out, calls for help, and is reassured by the comfort and presence of the parent who says, "Don't worry. I'm here. You had a bad dream." Nevertheless the images have come from somewhere, from some unidentified fear, and the wise parent will gently enable the child to be in touch with the real issue which gave rise to the dream. God listens to all the irrational, exaggerated recital of "enemy activity" in our lives, and enables us to distinguish between the specters created by our paranoia and the real foe who threatens us. Psalm 55 is a good example of the way in which God deals with one person who describes the breakdown of all that makes for security in his life, pointing at so many sources of pain, but ultimately arriving at the real issue. A close friend has failed him, and that makes the whole world seem out of kilter.

Jeremiah plumbs the depths of despair in the last of the confessions (Jer 20:14–18). No ray of light penetrates to mitigate the darkness of this cry of defeat in which he curses the day of his birth and the bearer of the news. It would have been better, he says, if he had died in the womb so that his mother's body became his grave. Perhaps few of us have prayed out of such total despair. Yet there must be a place in which to express the annihilating hopelessness that leads some to curse their own birth—even to take their own lives. There must be such a place if we hold fast to the conviction that God is merciful and that God is the redeemer of all, even the grossest human darkness. Jeremiah lived, but not without passing through the most excruciating pain of dereliction in the face of what appeared to be a meaningless existence.

Some years ago I was talking with a woman at the edge of despair. She was in the process of a painful divorce, without a regular job, and finding many obstacles in the way of pursuing her chosen vocation. As one who had meditated for many years, it was particularly stressful to discover that she could no longer experience the sustaining presence of God through meditative silence. In fact communication seemed to have broken down. Since she was experiencing only anger, disappointment, humiliation and a desire for revenge, there seemed to be nothing to say to God, and God appeared to be absent from her. The breakthrough came when she began to pray her rage, not in conventional ways, but through movement. As a dancer she often expressed the more peaceful dimensions of prayer through body movement, but had not considered expressing the pain of the present in this way. Dance enabled her to give voice to all the disappointment, the anguish and the doubt that besieged her, and, ultimately, to find healing.

Our image of God frequently needs expansion. Most often we need to let go of the censuring parent figure before whom we have to curb our real desires and angers. Such an image suggests that the creator is only interested in a limited area of our lives: that in which we are tranquil, compliant and always smiling our acceptance of the way things are. Jeremiah introduces us to God as a conversation partner with whom no topic is forbidden and no emotion too much to handle. This God treats us as adults, not taking responsibility for fixing everything, but pointing to ways of living in and through adversity. Sometimes God is silent. Learning to live with those silences is, perhaps, the hardest lesson of true prayer. Jesus in Gethsemane agonized over his sense of where his vocation was taking him and begged for its consequences to be removed. In God's eloquent silence he finally found the courage to say "Not my will but yours be done," and it was said with no divine reassurance that all would be well in the end.

We also need to recall often that God is the God of history, not only in the broad terms of human history, but of our personal history as well. A frequent word in the scriptures is "Remember." Remember all the way the Lord your God has led you; remember the rock from which you were hewn; do this in remembrance of me. We need this reminder because, as the old hymn puts it, "I forget so soon." In adversity and in ecstasy the temptation is to forget the interventions of God in our lives, those special moments when we stood breathless as we experienced the divine presence transforming our experience. We forget, too, that our call is rooted in God's word and choice. Jeremiah in his most desperate moments needed to be reminded that his ministry was, in fact, God's. He needed to recall the promises that accompanied the call in order to find the strength to go on. Escape was no answer. Like St. Paul, struggling many centuries later with his "thorn in the flesh" he found no magic formula for making the pain go away. Instead, "remember." To Paul the word came: "My grace is sufficient for you, for my power is made perfect in weakness" (2 Cor 12:9). No doubt that word enabled him to remember the many past experiences of God's grace, poured out upon him in moments of great need. It is a word from God to us in our helplessness and fear.

There was nothing static about Jeremiah's relationship with God. A robustness characterizes his thinking, and he dares to move out of assumed patterns of relationship. He engages actively, often in combat, with his maker and yields up his demand for equilibrium when it is in danger of becoming idolatrous. A friend of mine once remarked wistfully to his religious superior that he longed for a plateau. He had just received distressing news about an acquaintance and was feeling that life was a series of mountains and valleys from which there seemed to be no respite. "You can have a plateau any time you want—it's called death!" was the reply. A substantial part of life is involved with tension and ambiguity. Vitality in ministry demands that this part of experience is not denied. It does not demand that we like it or accept it in an uncomplaining way, but that we learn to be present to it, allowing God participation in all its anguished cries. That is to opt for life.

Through his confessions Jeremiah invites us to journal the bad news as well as the good news about our situation. It takes courage to step outside the parameters of traditional religious piety in order to engage with a God who disappoints, angers, and sometimes remains silent to us. It means laying ourselves open to jeopardy and risking the whole enterprise of discipleship. The alternative, while appealing, is, in the end, disastrous. If we yield to our fear of losing the comfortable, domesticated God of our imagination, the spirit within us shrivels into a withering and lifeless thing. The plateau is a barren place unin-

habited except for the ghosts of fear, sloth and unreality.
There is struggle on the mountains and in the valleys, and
that is the most convincing evidence of life.

Journal Exercise

Read the little book of Jonah. This prophet did not
want God to be "Lord of hosts" and resisted sharing the
message of hope to those he did not want included among
the covenant people. Reflect upon his thinking and his
actions. Do you find any parallels in your own experience?
Are there those who are outsiders to you? Do you sometimes feel the resentment he expressed at the end of the
book? Journal with your response.

8

Embracing Ambiguity

When Jeremiah had come to the dungeon cells, and remained there many days, King Zedekiah sent for him, and received him. The king questioned him secretly in his house (Jer 37:16–17).

One of the major questions highlighted by the experience of Jeremiah is: "Are the promises of God adequate?" In view of the conflict he endured, and the continuous misunderstanding, what does he have to say about the worthwhileness of his commitment to God's call? As we have already seen he frequently complained, accused God of desertion, and wished to escape, yet the very existence of the book which bears his name testifies to his "yes" to life. Sometimes the promise was forgotten and he sank into the pit of despair, but again and again, in his struggle with chaos and confusion, he found fresh hope. Clarity, "success," equilibrium were not generally present, but he learned to live in the gray areas of life where there are no answers, only layers of foggy uncertainty.

Living with ambiguity is never easy. We want clarity, a plain path, a route which is definitive, and a God who is always there to point the way when choices present themselves. When these things are lacking there is a temptation to believe that something has gone wrong, or that we have gotten off on a false trail. We want God to rescue us and to take away the discomfort of being confused. But faithful

living of our call is not like that. The conflicts we experience and the obscurities we have to face are a normal
aspect of authentic life. They do not indicate that somewhere we "went wrong" but, on the contrary, point to an
affirmation of our willingness to risk ourselves on the
promises of God.

One of the most confusing, frightening times I have
ever lived through occurred when the faith structure
which had felt secure fell apart and I no longer knew what
I believed or where I was going. For many years member-
ship in a fundamentalist church had given me an identity, a
way to interpret scripture, and a great deal of affirmation.
Gradually, however, my study of theology and life experience led me to question many of the assumptions of this
kind of thinking. At first I buried the questions. It was too
painful to engage in the work of "pulling down and plucking up"—much safer to leave the edifice intact. As time
went on I sensed that the foundations were becoming
more and more shaky. I simply could not go on denying
the questions because, in the process, I was denying a
large part of my own identity. I had to let go of the security
of an authoritative system which told me what to believe
and how to behave and, instead, opt for risk.

One of my leisure activities at this time was rock
climbing, and at the end of each day on the mountains a
group of us would sit around the fire telling hair-raising
stories of moments when we seemed to be hanging on to a
cliff only by our fingernails! I remember thinking of this as
an analogy of what was happening to me spiritually. I felt
myself to be in a very precarious place, roped to the lead
climber but filled with doubts about the security of the
rope and the trustworthiness of the lead. Did I still have a
connection with the God who called me to faith? Would
that God now abandon me because I dared to doubt, ques-

tion and, like a small child, push love to its limits? As I stayed with the chaotic uncertainty and faced into the fear of loss, I occasionally glimpsed some new possibilities for faith. At the same time I began to lose friends, especially among those who had been with me as part of the inner circle of "sound" believers.

Perhaps the most difficult part of this experience was that there was no new place to go—at least I had not yet discovered one—so the loneliness of my position was acute. I did not really belong with any group, and my connection with God seemed tenuous, yet oddly strong. Maybe this experience was closely related to what Kierkegaard calls the leap of faith—a leap into darkness or into the abyss—and I did not yet know that I would eventually touch down on solid ground. I wanted an end to ambiguity, yet somehow I knew that where I was was where I needed to be. It was the right place. A book came my way at this time and provided a revolutionary new insight that helped validate what I was going through. It was called *Tensions,* and was subtitled *Necessary Conflicts in Life and Love.* Written by Harry Williams, former Cambridge don, now a monk with the Community of the Resurrection, it made plain that conflict is inevitable if we really choose life and it is not evidence of something having gone wrong with us. Like Jeremiah I began to hope again. Eventually it would be time to build and to plant, but it was necessary to be in the dismantling process for the present.

From the womb Jeremiah was destined to be a cause of conflict and to live a conflicted personal life. In his early days at Anathoth he may not have been aware of this dimension of his call, but it was there. He did not start out with life all put together and then take some direction which made it fall apart. He was simply living his way into

God's will for him and discovering as he went that this meant considerable ambiguity would accompany his journey. Risk was a major theme in his ministry and experience, and it is a fundamental aspect of the life of faith. We are called to faith in God who is a risk-taker; we are not called to safe dogmatic systems which dehumanize us into puppets and which become idolatrous in their bland certainty.

The first creation story in Genesis 1 is a story of risk. God speaks into the chaotic darkness and begins to bring order and to give each created thing its time and place. Finally human beings are created in the divine image, and another risk takes place as they are entrusted with the stewardship of the earth. God risks each time new leaders or prophets are raised up, for they are all vulnerable and fallible human beings, entrusted with a task. The opening chapter of St. John's gospel, closely related to the Genesis story, speaks of God's ultimate risk. Into the darkness and confusion God comes as the Word which brings life—the Word which becomes flesh and dwells among us. This is God's great "yes" to ambiguity, for God enters it and lives it.

Journal Reflection

Think back over your life and try to identify times when you were particularly aware of making changes that left you feeling alone, confused or uncertain. How did you deal with these situations? Journal your response. Next take some time to explore your feelings about the ambiguity you experienced. Instead of using words, try to dialogue with the feelings using shapes and colors. A box of crayons and some large sheets of paper can provide a wonderful way of getting in touch with buried emotions.

Now consider your relationship with God at this time. Begin a dialogue with God and include in the conversation any questions and uncertainties with which you are dealing.

Doubts in the Darkness

Chapter 37 of the book of Jeremiah describes the experience of the prophet shortly before the exile. Jeremiah was sent by God to warn Zedekiah that the lifting of the siege by the Babylonians was only temporary, and that the Egyptian forces who came to aid Judah would soon withdraw. At this time Jeremiah attempted to return to Anathoth to "receive his portion," an obscure statement which may refer to the land deal he later completed in prison. At the Benjamin Gate he was accosted, the sentry refused to believe his story, and he was thrown into jail as a deserter. He remained there until his appeal to Zedekiah, when he was allowed to live in the court of the guard and given a loaf of bread to eat each day. His liberty taken from him, Jeremiah was forced to face even more poignantly the ambiguity of being a servant of the all-powerful Lord of hosts while he felt powerless and alone.

Six centuries later another uncompromising, robust figure found himself incarcerated in a subterranean dungeon near the Dead Sea. John the Baptist, a desert dweller and rugged preacher of repentance and judgment, had also interfered in political events and was paying the price. Shortly before he was murdered at the whim of the angry wife of Herod, he agonized over the truth of his message. Was Jesus truly the Lamb of God who takes away the sin of the world, or did John get carried away by his enthusiasm for the new preacher and healer? Doubts were his constant companions in that place of oppressive darkness. What he had said and believed in the open no longer made any sense, and no voice from the sky told him what to do. So he sent word to Jesus: "Are you he who is to come, or shall we look for another?" (Lk 7:19). Jesus' reply was to point out the evidence—lives changed, bodies healed, the liberating gospel proclaimed. It was no reassuring "yes" but rather the offering of data on which John could make up his mind. Ambiguity was not taken away; he still had to process the information and decide for himself.

John the Baptist went to Jesus with his question. Jeremiah turned to God, sometimes in anger, sometimes in anguish, as he wrestled with confusion and confronted fear. In that time of disorientation I described earlier, I did not give up on prayer but found that it needed to take new forms. Much of the time words were inadequate, and it was then that I discovered the value of silence. It was both frightening to stop talking to or at God, and also a relief to let go of the words that so often seemed to get in the way. It was hard to be in silence and to wonder if I would ever again "hear" God's voice, and a relief not to be hearing my own! In the silence I learned something of who I was and what I learned came from a deeper source than the voices that had defined me in terms of their system of thought. I also began to understand a little of the meaning of the psalmist's injunction, "Be still, and know that I am God." In stillness the intangible, indefinable God *was,* I *knew,* though I could have explained nothing.

Journal Prayer

Set aside some time to experience silence. It is not easy simply to move into a silent place, so prepare for it in the way you find most helpful, e.g. listening to meditative

music, using relaxation exercises, breathing deeply. Begin
with just a few minutes and notice what happens when
you try to be still. In your mind begin repeating the words,
"Be still, and know that I am God," or say them aloud if
that feels right. After you have said this mantra prayer
twenty times, return to the silence. Be aware of your feelings and of any images or thoughts that emerge. Write of
the experience in your journal. You can repeat this exercise over a period of time, increasing the number of
minutes you give to it as you go along.

Who Am I?

One of the reasons ambiguity is so hard to deal with
today is our education into either-or, dualistic thinking.
We are taught to be analytical, to categorize and to define
exactly what is or is not true. We learn to operate from the
left side of the brain but, sadly, neglect the wisdom which
comes from the more intuitive, creative right side. Jeremiah encourages us to deal with both-and, with con-
nectedness, and with not always making rational sense.
Theology has much to learn from contemporary physics
where more space is given to mystery and to ambiguous
items of data about which the researcher needs to remain
open. We are often afraid of the Mystery at the heart of the
universe, and so try to explain who and what God is. Jeremiah did not understand. Like us, he had only a limited
amount of information and experience on which to base
his ideas about God, and so he lived with many unsolved
questions. We need the humility of openness—the willingness to change our perceptions as we grow, and to be
confused in the process.

Jeremiah not only found that ambiguity characterized
his relationship with God, but he was also an enigma to

himself. The further he went in his obedience to the divine call, the less he was able to say: "This is who I am." The person he thought he was began to change, and went on changing though his basic personality type remained the same. Who am I? Forthright preacher of judgment? Comforting pastor? Village idiot? Heretic? Prisoner? Landowner? Prophet? Priest? Am I a contemplative? Paranoid? Optimist? Pessimist? Introvert? Depressive? God's person or one who acts out of a perverted sense of my own importance? It was not possible to choose one designation at the expense of all others. Jeremiah was a complex human person, sometimes acting in harmony with his own preferred mode of being, and sometimes stepping out into uncomfortable places for the sake of the truth as he understood it.

Problems arose when others tried to stereotype Jeremiah into particular roles and behavior patterns. "We don't do things like that here" was the clear message when he went public and shockingly visual in his proclamation of doom on Jerusalem. He made a scene when he broke the pot and walked about wearing a yoke like some harnessed ox, and his people were highly embarrassed. "We have experts to instruct us" was what he heard when he dared challenge the political and religious thinking of the time. "You don't fit in the family system anymore" was implied by his relatives as he lamented his ostracism by them. Bigger problems arose when Jeremiah was tempted to stereotype himself. It was his anguished asking of the question Who am I? that led to the confessions with their despair and lostness.

As I stepped outside the familiar patterns and definitions I too received many messages about the inappropriateness of my different response to life. I was no longer acceptable to those who had the answers already assured

and who would tolerate no deviations from biblical liter-
alism. Uncertainty was not an option for them, and as long
as I expressed any I did not belong. The "experts" made
several attempts to set me straight, but their fear tactics
did not work anymore. I was free and, at the same time,
scared and exhilarated by that freedom. However there
were moments of great self-doubt, and these were much
more difficult to deal with. Suppose those who now rejected me were right? What if I never again found a secure
faith? Since I no longer fitted the category of compliant,
dependent, submissive woman, how could I define myself? Was I heretical, liberal, Protestant, Catholic, pastoral,
prophetic, gracious or strident?

Either-or did not work. The truth was that I am a mixture of many emotions and of clear and fuzzy thinking. In
that ambiguity I had to live, and still have to live. My vows
as a priest in the Episcopal Church demand that I uphold
its doctrine and respect its hierarchy, yet I have to wrestle
with what seems at times an inadequate interpretation of
that doctrine and an abusive exercise of power. Is it the
moment to be pastoral or prophetic, compliant or asser-
tive, to accept a decision with which I do not agree or to
challenge it? Since I chose not to be a parish priest, I don't
fit well into perceived notions of what a priest is. At times
I celebrate that—we need new models and fresh ways
of thinking—but sometimes it is hard to be "different."
Above all I don't want to "make a scene" because I know
what happens to people who get too serious about their
convictions!

Embracing ambiguity is a necessary aspect of spiritual
growth, but it should not be confused with a refusal to
struggle with questions and uncertainties. There is a kind
of idle remaining in chaos, a preference for muddle over
the hard work of discernment, which is deadly in terms of

our human journey. Jeremiah could not be accused of this, but he did learn to let go of the demand for equilibrium and to accept the unanswered state of things. The book does not have some fairy tale "happily ever after" ending tacked on. As far as we know Jeremiah went to his grave with many of the issues unsolved and still wanting to resist the more painful parts of his call. But he did go on, and he did know a continuing relationship with God, albeit a stormy one at times.

There is a story that the Hopi Indians tell their children. When you wake up in the morning, they say, the first thing to do is hum home your shadow. You have a shadow which follows you wherever you go during the day, but at night it is free and takes off on its own adventures. However, you have a hum which only your shadow knows, and as soon as you hum it, the shadow must return. If you forget to do this, you may begin to feel you got out of bed on the wrong side, but really the problem is that you are missing your shadow. There is much wisdom in this story. We have a source of wisdom, our unconscious, which often addresses us through dreams and is available to us during the day if we will but pay it attention. Getting to know this shadow part of ourselves enables us to better understand who we are and to trust our own sense of direction. It is the part of our being that encourages us to take risks, to act and speak in contrast to prevailing attitudes, and to believe that God does work through the interior wisdom with which we have been endowed.

In many ways it is more attractive to rely on external authority figures for our sense of security, but this can be a fearful way of short-circuiting our connection with the Source of all wisdom. I am not suggesting that our journey has to be, or should be, undertaken in isolation from others or that we should relinquish all support systems.

We need each other, and God has provided a community in which we live and grow. But if we cease to take any responsibility for growth, refusing the risk of trusting our sense of direction, then we may be opting for stagnation. Jeremiah did have the faithful Baruch with him during most of his ministry. During my own period of searching and uncertainty I found a wise spiritual director, who did nothing to relieve me of the ambiguity but provided much encouragement to go on. He did not become another authority figure telling me how to behave and what to think, but he was there as a discerning friend to support me in the chaos.

Embracing ambiguity means giving up the myth that one day we will have it all together and everything will become clear. As long as we are on this earth we will be subject to the confusions, the paradoxes and unsolved questions which are an inevitable accompaniment of being human. This does not mean that we have somehow got onto the wrong track; rather it indicates that we have opted for reality with all its frustrations and possibilities, instead of clinging to simplistic explanations and rigid structures. It means that, like Jeremiah, we have chosen life.

Journal Questions

1. How would you describe yourself? Are some aspects of your life in conflict with others? How do you feel about that?

2. Have there been wise friends in your experience, people who have supported you but left you free to discover your own way?

3. Do you have such a person now? If you do, describe him or her and consider what you want to say the next time you meet. If you do not have such a support person, you might want to consider finding a spiritual director/ guide to journey with you and provide some perspective on the way.

9

Faith and Falsehood

And the Lord said to me: "The prophets are prophesying lies in my name. I did not send them, nor did I command them or speak to them. They are prophesying to you a lying vision, worthless divination, and the deceit of their own minds" (Jer 14:14).

We have a tendency to prefer a certain amount of illusion because the naked truth is often starkly uncomfortable. Those who nudge, or sometimes thrust us into seeing the difference between reality and our blurred notions of it, are not easy to live with. They generate hostility because they challenge the structures we erect to convince ourselves that our view of things is right. Peeping out from these solid edifices through the tiny windows which allow only minimal vision, we tell ourselves that we have no need for the strident voice which reaches us from "outside" and calls upon us to think again. Jeremiah certainly was such a voice in his day, making a clear separation between faith and falsehood, and shaking the structural foundations of his society.

God made it clear to Jeremiah that the national prophets were dealing in falsehood. There is a certain satisfaction to be derived from hearing that others are wrong, though it carries its own danger. All too easily a

self-righteous superiority can be embraced until it becomes an equally insidious idol setting us apart with a
sense of our own "rightness." However Jeremiah found
the awareness acutely painful because he was again called
to costly prophetic action, engendering once more the
anger and rejection he feared. By his call Jeremiah was
summoned by God to tell the truth. It was not a question
of "getting the message" and delivering it once and for all,
but of being involved in a continuing process of discernment, expressing in different ways and contexts the challenge of God's word. Jeremiah himself was in process and,
as we have already seen, conflict was inherent in the nature of his ministry.

So Jeremiah perceived the reality of God in very different terms than those of his contemporaries. In their
minds the question of God was closed. God was the pro-
tector of Judah, enshrined in the temple, law and sacral
kingship, none of which could be shaken despite evidence
of Babylonian expansion. God had been defined, and, in
the process, rendered timelessly tolerant toward the covenant people and ever destructive toward those peoples
who were outside the faith of Israel. It was easy to project
all evil and falsehood onto the "pagan" nations surround-
ing the chosen people. On the other hand Jeremiah spoke
of a holy God whose power and compassion reached far
beyond national boundaries. He recalled people to faith,
demonstrated by moral living, and from the falsehood of
complacency. His was a call to fresh vision, to leave the
idolatry of empty religion, and to allow God to be rede-
fined and to come disturbingly close.

The kings of Judah embodied promise—the promise
that through the line of David God would bless and protect the people. They held considerable power and gave
definition to those they governed and so carried heavy re-

sponsibility to live in truth as Yahweh's representatives. Several times Jeremiah takes issue with kings who have lost sight of the duty they bear in view of their sacred trust.

> Woe to him who builds his house by unrighteousness, and his upper room by injustice; who makes his neighbor serve him for nothing, and does not give him his wages; who says, "I will build myself a great house with spacious upper rooms," and cuts out windows for it, paneling it with cedar, and painting it with vermilion. Do you think you are a king because you compete in cedar? (Jer 22:13-15).

Jehoiakim had failed to exercise true kingship. A just administration makes the king, not a fancy palace designed after the style of the Egyptians. He lived and reigned in falsehood and will be rejected by God.

King David was a shepherd, and those who inherited his throne were to be shepherds of God's people. Instead they destroyed and scattered the sheep, so Yahweh threatened to deal with them for their betrayal of trust, and, at the same time, to save a remnant of the suffering flock (Jer 23:1-4). Jeremiah speaks out against falsehood and injustice in high places, challenging the bearers of power and by his words calling into question the reality of their authority. Six centuries later Jesus stands before Herod and unmasks the pretender by his silence (cf. Lk 23:9). His non-response to this lightweight, doubtful claimant to the throne of David is more eloquent than words, especially as the derision and physical abuse continue. Before the Roman governor, Pilate, Jesus makes some response but leads the questioning toward a discussion of the nature of power. As the gospel writers continue the narrative, Pilate diminishes and the full stature of Jesus becomes clear. Pilate may sentence him to death, but has no ultimate power over him. It is a question of truth and falsehood, real and imagined power. The author of the fourth gospel constructs the narrative to make this even more clear. From the outset Jesus is seen as the judge, Pilate and his accusers are in the dock, and the reader is left in no doubt about where real authority lays.

Jeremiah must have frequently clung to God's promise to make him "a fortified city, an iron pillar, and bronze walls, against the whole land, against the kings of Judah" (Jer 1:19), and often have felt far less fragile than these images suggest. In earlier chapters we looked at his laments, the anguish of his confessions, and his questioning of whether the promises of God were able to sustain him through so much suffering. Jesus, too, struggled with the cost of vocation. In the wilderness he was invited to choose falsehood and so to lose himself by aligning his mission with corrupt power. In Gethsemane he shrank from the terrible consequences of faithfulness. To Peter he said, "Get behind me, Satan," when the apostle suggested escape instead of unflinching obedience to God's truth. The continuing struggle between truth and falsehood is inherent in the call of God to people in all time.

In most false claims there is an element of truth. The people of Israel became a covenant nation and so enjoyed the privileges of a close relationship with God. They were unique. The temptations of Jesus were framed in the words of scripture; they were true, up to a point. It is when partial truth is made into an ultimate claim about the way things are, without any reference to context or integrity, that idolatry happens. The domesticated God of Judah was idolatrous, because justice and faithfulness were lacking, and these too were an essential part of the covenant relationship. Truth is not a possession which some people hold exclusively to support their view of things. Truth is uncomfortable; most of the time we only glimpse it and often we want to reject it.

Journaling with Imagination

The gift of imagination provides a way of entering into a deeper awareness of the relationship we have with God. Take some time to relax, become centered, and still. Close your eyes and ask yourself the question, "How does God see me?" Allow yourself to see in detail the person God sees. What are you wearing? Where are you? What are you doing? Is anyone else present? Notice your surroundings. What kind of day is it? How do you feel about the person God sees? When you are ready, record in your journal any insights that emerge from this exercise. Were there any surprises about God's view of you? Note the true things about yourself which were evident. If you were aware of any false or insincere aspects of your character, consider what you want to do about them.

Truth and Falsehood in Today's World

In the early 1970s I lived and worked in South Africa. I knew a good deal about apartheid from white South Africans I met in England and from writers like Alan Paton. I believed it was wrong, but nothing prepared me for the shock of living with the reality of what is euphemistically called separate development. I would find myself in the wrong line in the post office, about to sit on the wrong seat at a bus stop, or trying to engage in conversation with a black servant conditioned to answer only what she thought I wanted to hear. In fact it never was a conversation, merely a required response to a superior white being. I became so accustomed to the "Whites Only" signs everywhere that when a local store had a "White" sale, I thought they were excluding the black customers on whose purchase of merchandise they relied, until I realized it was a reference to a sale of linens!

I felt angry, impotent, and scared. I also enjoyed a high standard of living, the security of a job, and a year in which to explore some of the most beautiful parts of Africa. And that meant I felt guilty. I was a member of a privileged minority, enjoying prosperity at the expense of a large, oppressed majority. My presence there was, in a sense, helping to maintain a false view of human dignity and I was doing nothing tangible to change the situation. One of the most disturbing discoveries was that, at the end of a year of censored newspaper and radio broadcasts, I was beginning to hear bits of "truth" about apartheid, the kind of "truth" that suggested change was impossible. It *is* true that many of the different black tribal groups are hostile toward each other, and so cannot co-exist or provide leadership that would unify. (It is also true that British missionaries first hit on the idea of separating the groups!) It *is* true to say that most blacks lack the education for leadership; it is also true that they have been denied the academic opportunities provided for white students. It *is* true that profound differences exist between white English-speaking South Africans and the Afrikaners who currently hold power in parliament. It *is* true that a sudden change in policy and government would almost certainly lead to chaos and bloodshed. But do all these bits of truth add up to the rightness of continuing a system which degrades, dehumanizes, and oppresses mil-

lions of persons created in God's image and destined to
inherit the liberty of the children of God?

Not all of us are called to stand before kings and
governments to call into question the false premises on
which they operate—though perhaps more are called than
respond. We can, however, find ways to express our solidarity with God's "anawim"—the poor, dependent and
disenfranchised members of our society. I can refuse to
buy products from South Africa or other countries which
continue to deny basic human rights—even though my
withdrawal of support may initially hurt those I want to
help. I can go on petitioning my own government about its
policies in relation to such countries, and I can register
my protest in the polling booth. I can find those close at
hand who are denied housing, education, jobs and commit
myself to changing the inequitable distribution of resources here at home.

Like Jeremiah we need to identify these major false-
hoods and take our stand against them, but an even more
demanding task faces us as we try to discern our personal
idolatries. If I can find falsehood somewhere else, I may
put enormous energy into opposing it and fail to recognize the compromises with truth which I make all too
easily. Perhaps this is especially true when it comes to
religious convictions and ways of worship. Some of Jeremiah's greatest conflicts came through the priests and
prophets of his time who saw themselves as guardians of
the truth. Jeremiah had wanted to be one of them, but had
been driven by his call and experience of God to stand
over against their claims to truth. Jeremiah's God was vigorous, disappointing, universally powerful, loving toward
enemies, not confined by temples, compassionate, and
surprising. God was not static, never seemed to be in the

same place twice or to leave the prophet comfortable with a sense that at last he had figured how to keep God from changing. Each time he thought that rest and reward might be forthcoming, his faith was stretched and God had to be rethought yet again.

This is iconoclasm. Those who commit themselves to the lifelong, arduous and infinitely rewarding task of discerning truth and reality will have their idols shattered continuously. Frightened people will cling to a view of reality that once sustained them. For many, the childhood image of God as the parent figure who fixes problems remains the predominant idol even in adulthood. That leaves them with big problems when God fails to act as they wish, and often leads to loss of any active faith. In the previous chapter I described the personal iconoclasm which took place when I risked allowing the many questions and doubts about the brand of religious certainty in which I grew up to surface. That dark and difficult period taught me that I am very prone to idolatrous images of God, and need to be shocked often into new ways of thinking.

Such a shock occurred a few weeks ago. Taking an early morning walk I noticed that the sun was making a string of flamingo colored clouds. It looked as though someone had trailed a huge feather boa across the sky, and I suddenly had the image of God, recently returned from a party, having tossed aside the boa before turning in! She must have had some party and now be sleeping soundly, I thought. Now this is a very inadequate, and inaccurate image of God. Scripture says nothing about feather boas and almost always uses a masculine pronoun when referring to God. Yet it does represent a truth sometimes forgotten. There is a real sense of play about God's work— read the first creation story if you doubt that—and a very clear portrayal of God as an artist, painting the sky, and making surprising things out of nothing. There are also many feminine images of God, many of them lost through the predominance of patriarchal thought forms and language. God is imaged as a mother eagle, as a bear robbed of her cubs, as a lactating woman, as wisdom offering her riches to those willing to receive them.

I have not started a new cult whose believers worship the boa God as the ultimate expression of truth. Mostly my thinking about God is pretty traditional. I am an Anglican, a Trinitarian, an Oblate in a Benedictine monastic house. That also means I am mostly quite serious about prayer and worship. I like routine, saying offices, reading large portions of scripture, attending the eucharist daily and sharing that experience with like-minded people. But I often forget to play. Relaxation sometimes gets squeezed out because I forget that being made in God's image includes the ability to laugh and create. And that walk was a timely reminder of the playfulness of God inviting me to explore my own ability to play. The all-serious God of my growing up years was as much a distortion of the truth about God as an exclusive adherence to the boa image would be. God is. At best we can speak in image and metaphor, but ultimately we will fall into idolatry if we make any one expression of God's reality into the only truth there is.

Jeremiah compels the people of his day to address the question of truth and falsehood in two basic but related areas—in relation to God and to social reality. His message is profoundly relevant to us in our very different time and culture. Our view of God will inevitably color our vision of society and our responsibility within it. For those who are of the opinion that the God question is settled, that they have already done all that is necessary to define

God's nature and influence, a static view of religion is likely to exist. The Bible may be read with diligence but more to support an already existing statement of belief than to be challenged into new ways of seeing. There will be little vitality to ministry and little awareness of the social implications of the gospel. The church in which I grew up was passionately biblical, but the Bible was explained and interpreted to us by the pastor, and any current issues were processed by him and pronounced upon. We were not expected to deal directly with the truth; it would be handed on to us and we were expected to then hold and promulgate it.

There was no social involvement or critique of inequitable systems of government in our church. That was not our business. If we got doctrine straight—and we spent a lot of time doing that—all would be well. We did support missionaries, but only those whose primary task was to evangelize, not those who were providing education, relief of hunger, or medical aid as their main ministry. Our God was entirely concerned with souls, and that view of God conditioned the view we held of social reality. God was more a derivation from Puritan theology than an independent reality vigorously challenging the construct of our lives. Jeremiah would not have been welcome in our midst any more than those who stepped outside the unquestioning acceptance of such teaching were while I was there.

There is another danger which is equally idolatrous. When activism becomes the sole preoccupation of religion, God is displaced or ignored. Very laudable social action can get divorced from relationship and from the sense of interdependence implied by the covenant relationship. Needs may be met but the deep desire for belonging left unfilled because those who did the rescuing are busy with a new cause instead of growing into community. The psalmist speaks of God "setting the solitary in families," and the basis of Israel's life was the compassionate care for one another which mirrored Yahweh's yearning over them. It was for this reason that the law formed the foundation of Hebrew faith. Though similar in many respects to other ancient law codes, the covenant between God and Israel differed in the emphasis placed on relationship rather than things. God's people were united to each other because they were related to the true God who asked for the first place in their lives. Anything less was idolatry. Doing good without reference to the author of all good can become a subtle form of human pride and arrogance.

Faith and falsehood. Faith is not simply believing in a set of creeds or a particular ideology, especially when that ideology is designed to support an existing style of behavior. Faith means risk; it means remaining open to the God who is always surprising us into new images and smashing up the old ones. It means trusting ourselves to live with questions and to refuse the ready-made answers that glide off the tongues of those who would have us adopt their view of things uncritically. It also means holding ourselves in readiness to respond by prophetic word and action so that the living, dynamic God becomes visible through us. Jeremiah speaks in startling ways about God and rattles the bones of tradition. Unless we choose falsehood we too will find new ways to pray, see, speak and live as we journal with him.

Journal Reflection

So many inequities exist in our world and in the local communities where we live. Reflect on whether God is

calling you to take a stand against some injustice or falsehood, and consider prayerfully how you might act. Journal
your thoughts.

Over the next few days ask the Holy Spirit to open
your eyes to fresh images of God's presence in the world.
At the end of each day take a few moments to ask yourself
how and when you have experienced the presence of
God, and respond with gratitude to the creator. When you
have concluded this reflection, again think through the
day, this time asking to see where you have missed opportunities to know and respond to God's presence. Then
write a brief prayer which summarizes how you feel about
the day, God, and yourself, and include a specific request
for whatever gift you need in order to be more fully alert
to the divine presence tomorrow.

10

Prayer in the Marketplace

Then in the hearing of all the people, Baruch read
the words of Jeremiah from the scroll, in the
house of the Lord, in the chamber of Gemariah
the son of Shaphan the secretary (Jer 36:10).

*M*any commentaries on Jeremiah have emphasized his
personal agony expressed in the confessions, and have
interpreted the prophet almost exclusively from the perspective of his private prayer. Jeremiah was a sensitive
struggler, intense, inward and often fearful in his response
to the divine call, but to view him only in these terms
falsifies the man, for it fails to do justice to the public
dimensions of his ministry. Jeremiah was involved with
civil and religious leaders, with lawmakers, with a corrupt
monarchy and with the specific political catastrophe
about to take place. He addressed big public issues which
religious certitude and national arrogance denied. He engaged in an exposé of the blindness which results from
settling for an uncritical, undemanding acquiescence to
the way things are.

Chapter 36 of the book of Jeremiah recounts one
of the most daring public declarations by the prophet
though he was prevented from being present to deliver
his message! As a persistent irritant to the religious authorities he had been barred from the temple, but God

had not ceased to speak to and through him. He was instructed to take a scroll and to record Yahweh's message
of condemnation along with the invitation to repent, so
that Baruch, Jeremiah's scribe, could read it before the
assembly. It was on the occasion of a solemn fast when
Jerusalem was crowded with pilgrims that Baruch first
read the scroll. Miciah reported the words to the state
officials who sent for Baruch so they too could hear the
message. They appear to have been supportive of Jeremiah and Baruch in this instance, for they told them to
hide, with the scroll, while its fearful message was relayed
to the king. Instead of heeding its warnings the king sent
for the scroll and contemptuously cut off each section as
it was read, tossing the words into a fire. There was no fear
and no repentance shown by the king and his servants.
Jeremiah had apparently failed.

God was not yet done with Jeremiah or the royal leadership. Once again the prophet was told to write the
scroll, this time adding a section on the rejection of
King Jehoiakim and his offspring. Although Jehoiakin, the
king's son, assumed the throne for three months, he was
quickly replaced by Zedekiah, the puppet king appointed
by Nebuchadrezzar of Babylon during the siege of Jerusalem. Jeremiah may well have expected that now he could
retire from public ministry, but it was not to be. Zedekiah
actually sent for the prophet to ask for his prayers and his
prediction about the future, an indication of the fear he
had of Jeremiah. Jeremiah counseled surrender to Babylon as God's purpose.

In these chapters Jeremiah stands in a very public and
unenviable position as God's prophet. The world of political and royal deception was exposed as he made clear the
realities of God's reign. Jeremiah did not deal in general-
ities, but took his place over against the existing power

structures and on the side of Babylon which he identified as agent of divine judgment. He saw beyond the present moment to a future when Babylon would triumph and found in that victory the future hope of Israel. Such remarkable vision of new possibilities could only come about through a willingness to see God's action in unlikely places and people. Jeremiah did more than observe the signs of the times; he held fast to a deep conviction of the sovereignty of God. The kings of Judah had ceased to be servants of Yahweh because they sought only personal ends, but, ironically, Nebuchadrezzar could be named God's servant (cf. Jer 25:9; 27:6; 43:10), since through him newness would come about. And Jeremiah recognized God's action in this upheaval.

As westerners we have become accustomed to a very privatized approach to prayer and worship which sometimes causes us to miss opportunities to see God's action in the public realm and to engage with it through prayer and action. Additionally, the attempt to separate church and state means that connections which need to be made between the two spheres are not made. A preacher who dares to call into question economic and foreign policies is likely to be criticized for mixing religion and politics. Any Christian who is vocal about inequities perpetrated by the company where she or he is employed will have a limited or uncomfortable tenure. Yet this is exactly the way Jeremiah operates. He *does* mix religion and politics, and would undoubtedly have a hard time comprehending the separation we attempt to make. Yahweh is a righteous God who demands justice and holiness, and who will use the peoples of the earth (not just a chosen few) to accomplish that purpose. The one who honors God must speak the word of truth that challenges, regardless of personal cost.

Jeremiah moves in and out of the private and public places as he learns to pray. In the honest lamentation and questioning of God, the confrontation between personal inclination and divine commission, he derived strength to be in public places. In the private encounter with God, there grew a conviction that the Holy One, the Lord of hosts, really does hold dominion and none can thwart the divine purpose. That knowledge drove the prophet into a world of crumbling power structures, where he stood as a witness to the unshakable rule of God.

We see a similar pattern in the life of Jesus. His struggle with temptation at the outset of his public ministry bears witness to the human desire to escape the cost of living as God's person. He hears an echo of the temptation in the words of Peter when the apostle suggests that the way of suffering is avoidable (Mk 8:33). In Gethsemane again he wrestles with fear, with mortality, and with longing for escape. At the moment when he says "Your will be done," he wins a massive victory for God and humanity. These private prayer struggles, and the frequent withdrawing from the crowds in order to listen to the voice of God, prepared him for his controversial and prophetic ministry. He taught with integrity and truth, surprising, upsetting, challenging those in power, supporting, nurturing and healing the weak and the poor. He enabled those with eyes to see, to re-vision the kingdom of God, and to begin to recognize not just its future aspect but its present reality.

This balance between public and private prayer is important for us too. We need the times of reflective waiting so that we may grasp afresh whose we are, and be reminded in times of international turmoil that we are "citizens with the saints and members of the household of

God" (Eph 2:19). In the space we give to silence, we also receive the summons to go out as witnesses to God's reign, and then we are likely to encounter resistance. That is the moment to name our fear, to ask for courage, and to entrust ourselves to the God who calls and keeps us in life. In this process maybe our understanding of prayer will also be expanded. Beyond the speaking and listening dimensions, prayer is also being. Often no words are necessary, because who we are speaks more loudly than any sermon, even when it is with knocking knees and a trembling heart that we take our stand in hostile places. But always we ask for the grace to be ready to speak when silence would be a denial of God's word to those who need to hear it.

Journal Exercise

Set aside some time to prayerfully read the newspaper. Ask God to show you signs of hope in the world and to reveal where brokenness exists because there is no recognition of God's reign. Offer prayer of intercession for specific people and situations that are mentioned, and then ask God to show you if there are ways in which you could be part of the healing process. Sometimes we feel overwhelmed because problems seem so big, but instead they can inspire some "smaller" action which can have an impact. If you read of a major oil spill polluting oceans and destroying animal life, your prayer may lead you into a commitment to a local action group trying to improve the environment. A story of refugee problems may call you to befriend a lonely person or recent immigrant. Accounts of bloodshed and inter-racial strife can become the inspiration for a peacemaking role among family, friends or the local community. At the end of this time of reading and prayer, record your thoughts in your journal, and include a note of any action you intend to take.

You might want to consider repeating this exercise on a weekly or monthly basis. It can also be a means of increasing awareness of God's involvement in all of life, and of consciously looking for signs of the coming of God's reign that call us to celebrate.

Prophetic Poetry

> Tired
> And lonely,
> So tired
> The heart aches.
> Meltwater trickles
> Down the rocks,
> the fingers are numb,
> The knees tremble.
> It is now,
> Now, that you must not give in.
>
> On the path of the others
> Are resting places,
> Places in the sun
> Where they can meet.
> But this
> Is your path,
> And it is now,
> Now, that you must not fail.
> Weep
> If you can,
> Weep,

But do not complain.
The way chose you—
And you must be thankful.[1]

This poem was written by Dag Hammarskjöld, former secretary general of the United Nations, on July 6, 1961. It
could have been written by Jeremiah in the year 587 B.C.,
for the experience it describes is the human experience
of aloneness, weariness, and a sense of needing to face the
destiny that is unique to each individual, especially those
called to public office. There is no indication in his book
Markings as to what international or personal crisis
Hammarskjöld may have been dealing with, but there is
enough in the poem to put us in touch with our personal
inner strivings and longings.

Jeremiah is a poet who offers to the world images that
are pregnant with life, waiting to be birthed in the imagination of his hearers. His language is "free, porous, and
impressionistic,"[2] and designed to awaken in others a
fresh vision which leads to action. He does not explain or
exhaust the meaning of his metaphors, for that would ren-
der them lifeless in the experience of others. His words
are timeless because each person must engage in a creative process in which imagination is the primary tool.
Jeremiah wants his nation to take seriously the threat of
the "foe from the north" imaged in the boiling pot of
Jeremiah 1:13, but the sense of relentless onslaught is
not all there is to see. In later writing he tries to suggest a
re-visioning of life, a new way of seeing the enemy as an
instrument of ultimate good in the hands of God, and he
wants to help the people of God face the pain that will
precede new life. By placing before them a "not yet" hope
for restoration, he enables the exiles to view their disorientation in a new way; it is not all there is; they have

the capacity to see beyond and to envisage a new national identity while living fully in the moment. Above all they can learn to see the world from the perspective of God's power.

Often poetic writing has an open-ended ambiguity about it which is tantalizing but, at the same time, the reason for its appeal, because we become part of the image by bringing our life history to it. Who were the ones resting in the sun while Hammarskjöld trod a more difficult way? I recall how often I have experienced resentment because others seemed to be on a permanent vacation while my path was strewn with boulders! Further reflection may put me in touch with moments when I too have experienced a time for resting, a refreshing interlude on life's journey, and I may want to give thanks. The poem may also invite me to consider carefully where I am at this moment on my pilgrimage and to pray the feelings that ask to be acknowledged. The wonderful thing about poets is that they trust their readers to continue the image in their own way and time.

Jeremiah had the insight to see that the inertia and complacency of his community came largely from lack of imagination. People had settled for a particular interpretation of God and the world. They were sure that the temple would stand forever; their prophets preached peace and they tried to deny the failure of Jerusalem from a civic and religious standpoint. Jeremiah invites them to see the failure and the coming destruction through word and action, and reveals the charade in which they are engaged. The worst kind of drama is being played out by those whose lives are devoted to protecting themselves and the nation from the truth that Yahweh is not derived from the continuing existence of the temple. The Lord of hosts, God of the whole earth, including Babylon, chooses to be known beyond the shrines erected to contain the deity and calls on Jeremiah to stand in the marketplace and smash old images, calling for a commitment to the creative task of re-visioning national identity.

Perhaps our greatest need today is for fewer closely reasoned sermons and more poetry. If the word from the pulpit does not activate the imagination of those in the pews, it does little to move God's people forward in their witness to the presence of the creator in the world. We have much to learn from the approach to scripture of liberation theology, in which the whole people of God is involved in the process of understanding, interpreting and living out the implications of the word, instead of leaving the responsibility for understanding to a select few authority figures. God has trusted each of us to be creators; we have tended to limit the wisdom of those without professional training, discouraging their attempts to make personal connections with the images of scripture. The authorities tried to limit Jeremiah too, and succeeded in some physical restraint, but the message was too powerful to silence. Six centuries later the successors of these religious leaders would try to silence a carpenter from Nazareth, questioning his credentials and scorning his teaching. In our day the power of that teaching, especially the images he uses in the parables, continues to stun us into new ways of thinking and acting as we allow them to enter our imagination.

What transformation might happen in our world if international leaders discovered the power of poetry to enable people to re-vision the future? We seem to base our whole defense strategy on increasing arsenals and preparing for war with the enemy in whom we locate evil. We hold on to the slogan "In God we trust" but feel that we must be capable of obliterating others in order for God to act on our behalf. Suppose, instead, we began to visualize a world at peace, and to allow our narrow interpretation about who are the people of God to be expanded? Maybe recent dramatic changes in the communist bloc countries are an invitation to rethink our attitudes and to find hope. We are engaged in a drug war. Is it possible that one of the ways to combat the destructive, dehumanizing effects of drugs would be to appeal to the creative imagination of those drawn into this means of escape from reality? What if children were allowed to create, play, discover the power of imagination to change lives, instead of being filled with facts which may prove to have little relevance and no inspiration for envisioning a different future? We spend so much time trying to contain or control problems that we have little energy left for the imagination to suggest fresh ways of looking at life so that the emptiness and futility which leads to despair can be addressed.

Becoming a Poet

Several years ago when I was serving as a priest in a large midtown Manhattan parish, a group of us took the train to Freeport, Long Island for a day of celebration, eucharist, and poetry. We gathered in a meadow close to the salt marsh, a mixed group of small children, grandparents, singles and families, and sat at picnic tables as Max Wheat, a local poet/naturalist, spoke to us of our ability to create poetry. Many of us were skeptical. We had never written a poem, had not received high grades in creative writing, and had experienced difficulty in trying to understand other poets. The enthusiasm and confidence of Max was catching, however, and after he had given us a four line verse to use as a model, inviting us to change nouns and verbs using things we saw around us, we began to see that our eyes and imagination were all we needed. From the same simple four lines, each of us communicated something about the day, our feelings and observations, and shared them with each other.

Soon we set off with notebooks to explore the marsh. We were instructed to write down anything that caught our attention, things we saw, smells, textures, sounds and the feelings generated by the environment. We observed a blue heron, egrets, numerous other marsh birds, sea creatures, wind blowing seeds, grasses, and all against a backdrop of the New York skyline! Returning to the picnic tables, we began to use these lists of observations as the starting point for writing. Our poems moved from simple description, to ideas and metaphors suggested by the things around us. For some the freedom of that wild and windy day suggested a contrast with the feverish pace of life in the city, where it was hard to find time to notice anything. Others focused on the simplicity of some of the growing things we saw, and reflected on ways in which they could draw us into choosing a simpler lifestyle. At least one person was in touch with the wonder generated by the intricate balance of the marsh creatures with their environment, and of the inter-connectedness of all living things.

Over a shared picnic lunch we continued to work on our writing, encouraging each other, asking for help when an image did not quite "work," and learning much from Max about the flora and fauna of the salt marsh. Our day ended with a celebration of the eucharist in which the homily was a sharing of all the creative work achieved that day. We heard poems by six year olds and by those in their eighties, and we delighted together in the variety of the images which came to help us re-vision our experience. For some this was the first experience of worship in the open air, and of a celebration of the eucharist where they could see the consecration of bread and wine happening in their midst instead of in a far distant sanctuary. The fact that our picnic table was now the altar helped us to reflect on the sacredness of all things, and we especially expressed gratitude for the sacred gift of creativity now expressed by each one.

In the first chapter of this book we looked at Jeremiah's experience of "waking up" to the power of God made evident in the simple images and objects that he observed. In the act of attention he saw more than a cursory glance would have told him; he saw truth about God and humanity. We become poets when we give time to what is there, instead of passing by the wonder of life and its capacity to reveal God to us. Poetry is birthed by those with open eyes and hearts, those willing to struggle with the difficult images, and those who respond to the call to share their vision in the marketplace.

Peter J. Ediger is a Mennonite pastor who now lives in Las Vegas, Nevada where he is co-director of the Nevada Desert Experience, a faith based organization seeking an end to nuclear weapons testing. Peter is a prophet and a poet. In many ways he reminds me of Jeremiah, not least because he refuses to find God only in comfortable places but opts for risk, questions, challenge, and worships One who is contemporary and deeply involved in all aspects of our politics and religion. His long poem "A Trilogy of Love"[3] moves in and out of the images of Gethsemane, Revelation and the Song of Songs, as it explores the tragedies and the possibilities of our time. There are three sections to the poem: Promise, Lamentation, New Creation. The following, so reminiscent of the marketplace preaching of Jeremiah, forms the central section:

1.
Groping his way between
cactus needles and olive branches
the One with the half-life leads us to
the garden of prayer where hell's superpowers
take on the Lamb of God who sweats
blood from every crevice in
the surface of the soul.
While we sleep
he wrestles with angels
O God I do not want to die
there are dreams not yet dreamed
there are dances not yet danced
O God I want to live
I want to live the other half of life
O God forbid that I should die
nevertheless
your will be done, not mine.

While we sleep his
story hangs in the balance.
While we sleep the demons pray.
In technocratic sanctuaries
demons worship metal gods
    Our power which rules the earth
    nuclear is your name.
    Our kingdom come, our will be done
    on earth and in the heavens.
    Give us this day our military superiority.
    And forgive us our vulnerability
    as we seek vengeance on all
    who threaten us.
    And lead us not into repentance

but deliver us from the evil empire.
for ours is the kingdom and the power
and the glory forever and ever amen.

The prayer of the demons
drives deep into the heart of the desert
explodes in the heart of the desert.
The desert night is dark.
We sleep.

2.
The whisper which will not be silenced
says
Open your eyes to that within.
Open your eyes to that without.
I see a beast with seven heads
stalking in the shadows of my soul.
I see a beast with seven heads
straddling seven seas
cavorting seven continents.
I hear the sobbing of a child
lost in the fearful secrets of my soul.
I hear the sobbing children of seven
continents crushed in arms of steel
children crushed in arms of the beast.
I weep.

I see the beast take on the guise of God
breathing benevolent blasphemies.
Follow me; I will offer you security.
Feed me; I will be your sure defense.
We feed the beast;
With millions, billions, trillions
we feed the beast.

We starve our child to feed the beast.
We starve the children of the world
to feed the beast.
I weep.

3.
Long have I heard your words O God
long have I learned your laws.
Now it is more than words I need
it is more than laws I want.
It is you my God my lover I want.
It is you I long for my lover my God.
All night long on my bed I look for you.
I look for you but do not find you.
All day long I search for you
in scripture and tradition
in doctrine and devotion
in sanctuary and in seminary.

Kiss me O God kiss me!
Kiss me with the kisses of your mouth!
Ravish me with the kisses of your mouth.

Do not arouse
or awaken love
until it so desires.

This poem speaks to me because it does more than offer statistics about our current dilemma. I am drawn into the pain of human arrogance, I mourn for the lost child within as well as for those who will never grow to maturity, I feel the emptiness of so much religious posturing, and I recognize that I am not simply an observer of this harrowing drama. I am involved. I must act, pray, be visible in the hostile places as I join with those who seek to offer an alternative vision and new hope for the world. And one of the means by which I can communicate an image of the new creation is through the pen.

Journal Suggestion

Set aside some time to go back to your earlier journal reflections following prayer with the newspaper. As you again think about the various reports and stories that caught your attention, ask yourself if any images strike you. Perhaps there was an account of an unscrupulous building developer whose greed resulted in loss of homes and harassment of poor families. Be aware of your feelings toward this person and toward those who were oppressed. Do you have any personal experience of being victimized by a person or institution, and of feeling powerless? Do other stories or biblical references come to mind? (I recall that King Ahab coveted the land belonging to his neighbor Naboth, and when he told his wife Jezebel, she had Naboth murdered and gave his property to her hus-band.) Jot down any ideas, thoughts, feelings that come to mind and think about what you want to say to society about this kind of behavior. Is there any one image that strikes you as a starting point for writing? Don't worry about rhyme, structure, coherence at this stage but begin to write what comes to mind, using the notes you have already made as you reacted to the story.

This kind of writing grows with time, especially if there is a person or a group with whom you can some-times meet to share what you have written. It might lead to the formation of a discussion/action group of like-minded people who commit to a regular time for reflection on scripture and its relevance to contemporary life and problems, and to the use of writing skills as a means of communicating alternatives to some of the destructive behavior in our society.

11

Endings

This is the number of the people whom Nebuchadrezzar carried away captive: in the seventh
year, three thousand and twenty-three Jews; in
the eighteenth year of Nebuchadrezzar he carried away captive from Jerusalem eight hundred
and thirty-two persons; in the twenty-third year
of Nebuchadrezzar, Nebuzaradan the captain of
the guard carried away captive of the Jews seven
hundred and forty-five persons (Jer 52:28–30).

How lonely sits the city that was once full of people! How like a widow has she become, she that
was great among the nations! She that was a prin-
cess among the cities has become a vassal (Lam
1:1).

*T*he second volume of Jeremiah's writings begins with a
lament which images the stark loneliness of the holy city
now desecrated and emptied of inhabitants. The end has
come. The age, which many thought would last forever,
has been brought to a close through the superior strength
of Babylon and the design of Yahweh. Jeremiah, who all
along predicted these events, does not sit down and smug-
ly bask in his vindication, but enters into the pain of God's
people at the loss of what was most dear to them. He feels

grief, mourns loss, and then, as we have already seen in chapter 5, becomes an agent of hope to the exiles. Jeremiah teaches us how to deal with endings, both the big public disasters and the private losses that are a normal part of human life.

The End of the Age

It is usually dangerous to draw precise analogies between one age and another, yet there are broad similarities between Jeremiah's time and our own. As we look at history, one of the most surprising discoveries is how little we seem to learn from past failures, for the same old patterns of aggression and imperialism are played out again and again. Jeremiah has some lessons for us if we are willing to feel the pain of his kind of vision of a world that is God's, and of our role as prophets who articulate a counter-cultural interpretation of human reality and relationships. We are beginning to hear the voices of such prophets in our day, even as we witness the dismantling of ideological national structures and hear the dying whimper of post-enlightenment certitude which sought to control through technological, psychological, political and religious knowledge. Our age also is dying.

John Shelby Spong, Episcopal bishop of Newark, titled his book on the future of the church *Into the Whirlwind,*[1] for he sees clearly that only those who are willing to brave the rigors of the storm-doubts in which old structures are challenged will have anything authentic to say to a disoriented people who long for hope. After exploring the dying of a religious certainty which is remarkably similar to the situation Jeremiah confronted in Judah, and the ending of many traditional patterns of human sexuality, Bishop Spong moves to what he calls the death, in our day, of tribalism and of "the tribal mentality that feeds such powerful emotions as nationalism and patriotism."[2] He goes on to say:

> Tribalism is the source of the hatred and fear that one nation articulates toward another nation or group of nations with which it competes for economic or military advantage. Tribalism is the content of our nationalistic propaganda. It is the basis upon which the world is divided into armed camps with each side willing to "defend" itself against the other. . . . The tribal mentality has a constancy that finds new incarnations in each moment of history, and through varying social and economic systems. . . . It is tribalism that makes us feel more secure when our weapons systems reach the absurd level of sophistication that will enable the efficient killing of every person in the world more than twenty times.[3]

Jeremiah says Babylon is in God's hands as much as beloved Judah, and will be the means by which Judah rediscovers her identity. Today we are compelled to rethink our convictions about national superiority as we learn to view the world as a global village and the peoples of the earth as brothers and sisters rather than enemies. And if we are tempted to look for a contemporary Babylon, we may find closer parallels in U.S. imperialistic posturing than in some distant "foe from the north."

Following the U.S. invasion of Panama in December 1989 a vigorous correspondence developed in the press as to the appropriateness of this action. The *National Catholic Reporter* of December 29, 1989, contained an article which was disturbing since it quoted a report of a "top secret" 1948 State Department document which, the author claimed, continues to influence foreign policy and our sense of national identity. We may be more cautious about making this kind of statement today, but, he asks, have our attitudes substantially changed?

> We have 50 percent of the world's wealth. But 6.3 percent of its population. This disparity is particularly great between ourselves and the people of Asia. In this situation, we cannot fail to be the object of envy and resentment. Our real task is to devise a pattern of relationships which will permit us to maintain this position of disparity without positive detriment to our national security. We will have to dispense with all sentimentality and daydreaming. Our attention will have to be concentrated on our immediate national objectives. We need not deceive ourselves that we can afford the luxury of altruism and world benefaction. We should cease to talk about vague, and for the Far East unreal, objectives such as human rights, the raising of living standards and democratization.[4]

Are there not some parallels here, too, as we listen to Jeremiah challenging the political presuppositions of Judah which left no room for the inclusion of others in God's rule? How might the creator be inviting us to restructure our thinking through such world events as the breaching of the Berlin wall, the surprising wind of change blowing through the communist world, and the increasingly persistent refusal of oppression by those who have been voiceless for so long and who are now being heard through such prophets as Bishop Desmond Tutu of

South Africa? Has God finally escaped from the confines
of a narrow, arrogant church and society which knew it
alone was right?

Journal Reflection

Vitality in prayer and Christian witness comes from an
awareness of the concrete ways in which God is active in
the world. Take some time to reflect on current world
events and to consider how these might be interpreted
from the perspective of God's reign. What old ways of
understanding are nearing death? How do you feel about
the loss of familiar patterns of thought? Are there questions and uncertainties which need to be spoken as you
wait for what is yet to come? Journal your response to
these questions. Conclude the exercise by telling God of
your hopes and needs as you accept change.

Julian of Norwich, the fourteenth century English
mystic, offers us an image in her *Revelations of Divine
Love* of everything there is held in the hands of God who is
a totally loving creator. As we deal with a rapidly changing
world and feel our responsibility for the "healing of the
nations," her insight can help us remain in touch with the
compassion of God which undergirds all our human caring. Our prayer and our action then flow from dependence on the ultimate love of God for all that God has made.
Read Julian's words and then place yourself in a relaxed
position. You might want to find a small, round object to
hold (hazelnuts are not always easy to come by) as a symbol of the world held lovingly in being by God. As you
allow yourself to become centered, bring the cares, needs,
questions into awareness and then slowly begin to repeat
Julian's words "All shall be well" as a mantra expressing
trust in the love of God. After you have repeated the man-

tra for ten minutes, move into silence, resting in God's care for you and for the world.

> And he showed me more, a little thing, the size of a hazelnut, on the palm of my hand, round like a ball. I looked at it thoughtfully and wondered, "What is this?" And the answer came, "It is all that is made." I marvelled that it continued to exist and did not suddenly disintegrate; it was so small. And again my mind supplied the answer, "It exists, both now and forever, because God loves it." In short, everything owes its existence to the love of God.[5]

Giving Time to the Pain

The contemporaries of Jeremiah blindly held to an ideology of continuity and blessing for Judah and masked the reality of the moment with slogans. "The temple of the Lord is inviolable," they claimed. "Peace, peace," they cried, when there was no peace (Jer 6:14). Jeremiah points out that they have applied bandaids to a deep and festering wound, refusing to deal with the real cause of sickness or even to recognize the seriousness of the symptoms. They were unwilling to deal with pain, to face their true condition, and so they opted for a quick and easy forgetting of the disease. Here too we find some parallels with our own time, not only in our dealings with other nations, but in an attitude toward discomfort which pervades all of our thinking. Our culture tells us that life is to be avoided by therapy, drugs, alcohol, or some other mind-numbing escape rather than faced and affirmed. Advertising suggests that there is a way out of every pain or problem, and usually the cure is associated with the word "instant."

"I haven't got time for the pain" says one of the advertising slogans for a particular brand of pain-killing medica-
tion; take me and your headache will disappear. The jingle
encapsulates current attitudes which deny the value of
pain and suggest that something is necessarily wrong with
anyone who chooses to pay attention to its lessons, not
out of masochism but from a willingness to process the
experience. Whether the pain be physical, spiritual or
psychological, God is able to lead us through to a place of
healing, but only if we stay long enough with the discomfort to allow it to teach us. Pain and loss are redeemable;
this is the message of Jeremiah, and it is a word we need to
hear in our day too.

Several years ago my cat had surgery, and when I
picked her up from the doctor's office, she was still in a
good deal of discomfort. Once we got home she found a
place on the carpet where she curled up and remained for
about twelve hours. My attempts to relieve my own distress by petting her and offering her favorite food were
met with a non-response. She was totally attentive to her
pain, to the present moment, and distraction did not
work. She taught me a lot, as she often does, by her commitment to reality. The speed of her recovery was remarkable too. Within two days she was climbing her favorite
tree and stalking birds. I try to remember her example
when I have a headache and am ready to reach for the pain
killer, when I feel the loss of a friend or of the presence of
God and instinctively turn to some form of forgetting. I
may well take the pain killer, but I also need to ask, "Why
do I have this headache? Is it because I need to pay attention to an over-full schedule, the lack of healthy exercise,
or a tense relationship which needs to be dealt with?" The
pill in itself is not the answer, though it may be a con-

sciously chosen means of relief as the real problem is addressed.

From the moment we are born, loss is a part of life which causes us grief. The separation from our mother's body evokes cries of distress, and our growth as autonomous beings happens through a series of separations and losses. Meister Eckhart once wrote that we grow by subtraction, not by addition; as we learn to let go of what is dear to us but no longer an appropriate way of being, we become more fully who we are meant to be. But the growth takes us through a process of grief which we are often tempted to curtail or avoid. We would rather not have to bid farewell to what is familiar and comfortable, and so we are tempted to prolong the moment and avoid the grief. Jeremiah suffered the loss of friends and family as he learned to become more and more fully God's person. He did not always endure the loss with grace, but as he poured out his distress, rage, and hurt, he found a way to allow these endings to be endings. And he found strength to go on.

The central section of St. John's gospel, chapters 14–17, contains the last words of Jesus as he prepared his disciples for his departure. It is presented in the form of a testament of the kind a dying rabbi would give to devoted followers who were to carry forward the essence of his teaching. These "Farewell Discourses" invite the disciples to enter into grief, to move on into a new phase of community, and finally to discover their own power for ministry through the Holy Spirit who will come to stand alongside them as Jesus had done. It is clear that they do not understand, but want to prolong the present situation in which they do not have to take responsibility for themselves. Jesus is insistent about the change that must happen, tells them that their pain will not last forever, and gives them a glimpse of the future which is bright with hope. He turns their despairing gaze from the past which is ending and he redirects their vision to the future with all its obligations. They are to reflect Christ's glory in a world which still opts for so much darkness, and in their witness they will discover a joy which far surpasses the sorrow that is part of human life in which loss is reality.

Learning to say goodbye is very difficult for most of us. Yet the very word implies that God is a part of the separation. "God-be-with-ye," we say, even as we let go of one deeply loved. We feel the pain and desolation of loss, and we commit the other into the care of God our loving creator. This is what Jesus did for the disciples. He looked at them with all their potential for good and with their foibles and fears, and he prayed for them as he committed them into the hands of the God he dared to call Father. Then he entered his own pain fully and consciously in Gethsemane, struggling through to the letting go moment, and entering the blackness of his last hours. The most impressive aspect of all the gospel accounts of the passion is the way in which Jesus was truly present in a caring way to all that followed from his moment of surrender.

Some of our losses are big ones. The death of a close relative or friend, whether through aging or tragedy, is an overwhelming experience from which we sometimes wonder if we will ever recover. But there are many smaller "deaths" which are less likely to claim our attention because they are not recognized as readily. I remember moving from one location and job situation to a new place where I felt fulfilled, happy and relieved. The earlier position had a great deal of stress associated with it, and at first all I could do was celebrate the freedom of this new way of life. Then I began, almost indiscernibly, to feel anxious and a bit depressed. My dreams were about moving, not being in a place I knew, trying to find my way. It took a while to realize that I had not in any way mourned the job and the city now left behind. In spite of the satisfaction of my new situation, there were losses associated with where I had been before, and relief at the change of place and pace had prevented me from seeing them and grieving.

A change of routine can bring a newness we celebrate, but may also mean that a familiar pattern of living is gone, and is cause for some grief. Changing patterns of health, even normal physical changes in our bodies, remind us of our mortality and invite us to mourn the passing of one phase in order to be able to enter into the joy of the next. A tree we regularly pass is gone one morning, and we feel its loss as we would miss a familiar friend. All these endings are material for prayer and journaling, and in the processing of the grief we find an invitation to newness. That was the message of Jeremiah. Out of grief, newness can come, and he preached with such conviction because he had learned to let go, to face loss, and to find God in the most difficult places human beings experience.

A Journal Exercise

Take some time to reflect on your life, the relationships that are current, your age, health, employment, and leisure activities. What is coming to an end for you? How do you feel about letting go of that which has been a part of your experience? Where will you find help as you enter into the grief process? Journal with your response to these questions. If it seems appropriate, use colors and shapes to represent your feelings at this time.

When you have completed the first exercise—and make sure you take as long as you need for it—ask yourself other questions: What is coming to life for you at this time? Where do you see newness in your experience, relationships, prayer? How do you feel about this? Again you may wish to use drawing/painting in addition to the journal activity. A particularly satisfying form of expression is the use of finger paints! Allowing ourselves to "regress" back to such kindergarten forms of art work wakes up the child in us who wants to create and celebrate new things.

Conclusion

In the process of journaling with Jeremiah we find many connections between the prophet and our own experience. Scripture is full of images and stories that enable us to see ourselves and to sense the commonality of all God's people who are journeying toward wholeness. The journey and the journal continue, and the God who led a fearful people out of bondage through the human agency of Moses sets us free as we walk into our future. Jeremiah introduced us to this way of traveling and others wait to teach us through their experience also. Another great story teller, who also uses poetic writing, is St. Luke, and reading his two volumes using the same journaling technique moves us into the breathtaking excitement of the early Christians as they learned to make sense of Jesus' death and resurrection.

Jesus is named the Word in the prologue of the fourth gospel because through him God speaks in a way we can understand. The Word became flesh, lived among us, shared all our human joy and pain. God goes on speaking and invites our response. Through the journal we enter into the process of listening to the God who speaks, and we learn to wait long enough with the life-giving Word so that we can respond out of a true heart-knowledge of who we are. God loves us, holds us in being, and gives meaning to all the glorious mixture of triumph and turmoil, dread and delight, fear and hope which make up our lives. We write our way into a deepening response to our creator who has gifted us with the healing power of words.

Notes

Preface

1. Edward J. Farrell, "The Journal—A Way into Prayer," chapter 2 of *Prayer Is a Hunger,* Dimension Books, 1972, p. 81.

2. Dietrich Bonhoeffer, *Letters and Papers from Prison,* SCM Press, 1968, p. 173.

3. Ibid.

Chapter 2

1. Francis Thompson, "The Hound of Heaven."

Chapter 3

1. Matthew Fox, *Illuminations of Hildegard of Bingen,* Bear & Co., 1985, p. 27.

2. Ibid., p. 28.

3. Daniel Berrigan, *The Discipline of the Mountain,* Seabury Press, 1979, pp. 60-61.

4. Walter Brueggemann, *Hopeful Imagination,* Fortress Press, 1986, p. 19.

Chapter 4

1. *A Monastic Breviary,* Holy Cross Publications, 1976, pp. 183-184.

2. J.A. Thompson, *The Book of Jeremiah,* Eerdmans, 1980, p. 228.

3. Thomas Merton, *The Sign of Jonas,* Harcourt, Brace & Co., 1953.

4. *The Church Times,* London, November 20, 1981.

5. Walter Brueggemann, "The Book of Jeremiah: Portrait of the Prophet," *Interpretation* Vol. xxxvii, No. 1, January 1983, p. 134.

6. Institute in Culture and Creation Spirituality Conference, Summer 1983, Holy Names College, 3500 Mountain Blvd., Oakland, CA 94619.

7. "The Ballad of Joe Hill," by Judy Russell and Gary Revel, The House of Talley Music Co. (BMI), quoted in *Choosing Life* by Dorothee Solle, SCM Press, 1981, pp. 83-84.

Chapter 5

1. Walter Brueggemann, *Hopeful Imagination,* Fortress Press, 1986, pp. 29-30.

2. Ibid.

3. Leon Joseph Cardinal Suenens, *New Pentecost.*

Chapter 6

1. Elizabeth Canham, *Pilgrimage to Priesthood,* S.P.C.K., 1983.

2. John Sanford, *Dreams: God's Forgotten Language,* Crossroad, 1968.

Chapter 10

1. Dag Hammarskjöld, *Markings,* Faber and Faber, 1964, p. 175.

2. Walter Brueggemann, *Hopeful Imagination,* Fortress Press, 1986, p. 23.

3. Peter J. Ediger, "A Trilogy of Love," in *As Tentative as Flight,* Graduate Theological Foundation, 1989, pp. 35f.

Chapter 11

1. John S. Spong, *Into the Whirlwind,* Seabury Press, 1983.

2. Ibid., p. 150.

3. Ibid., p. 151.

4. Thomas Gumbleton, "Invasion of Panama Further Evidence of U.S. Imperialism," *National Catholic Reporter,* December 29, 1989, p. 20.

5. Julian of Norwich, *Revelations of Divine Love,* Penguin, 1966, p. 68.